BUDDHISM

IS NOT WHAT YOU THINK

BUDDHISM

IS NOT WHAT YOU THINK

Finding Freedom Beyond Beliefs

STEVE HAGEN

HarperOne
An Imprint of HarperCollins Publishers

Some chapters, in slightly different form, previously appeared in the following publications:

"Time and Now" in *Tricycle*. Copyright © 1996 by The Buddhist Ray, Inc.

"Why Seek Liberation?," "No Mystery," "*This* Will Never Come Again," "The Itch in Your Mind," "Neither Sacred Nor Profane," "Liberation, Not Resignation," "The Most Valuable Thing in the World," "Truth Is Nothing Particular," "The Revelation of the World," "Nothing Else," "It's Enough to Be Awake," "How to Be Liberated on the Spot," "Paradox and Confusion," and "Canyons in a Cup" (under the title "Wake up!"), in Dharma Field Zen Center newsletter. Copyright © 1999, 2000, 2001, 2002, and 2003 by Dharma Field.

HarperCollins books may be purchased for educational, business, or sales promotional use. For information please e-mail the Special Markets Department at SPsales@harpercollins.com.

HarperCollins Web site: http://www.harpercollins.com

HarperCollins®, 📖®, and HarperOne™ are trademarks of HarperCollins Publishers.

FIRST HARPERCOLLINS PAPERBACK EDITION PUBLISHED IN 2004

Library of Congress Cataloging-in-Publication Data
    Hagen, Steve
    Buddhism is not what you think : finding freedom beyond beliefs / Steve Hagen.
        p. cm.
    1. Buddhism—Doctrines.   2. Truth (Buddhism).   I. Title.
    BQ4570.FH34   2003
    294.3—dc21   2003050812

ISBN 978-0-06-073057-4

HB 01.16.2023

To all my students

CONTENTS

PART 2: PURE MIND

PART 3: PURELY MIND

The foolish reject what they see,
not what they think;
the wise reject what they think,
not what they see.

—Huang Po

PROLOGUE

SEE FOR YOURSELF

*People say that practicing Zen is difficult, but there is a
misunderstanding as to why. It is not difficult because it is hard
to sit in the cross-legged position, or to attain enlightenment.
It is difficult because it is hard to keep our mind pure and
our practice pure in its fundamental sense.*

—Shunryu Suzuki

THIS IS NOT a feel-good self-improvement book about
how to become more spiritual. It's an intensely practical
book about how to live our daily lives openly and honestly,
with wisdom and compassion. It's a book about being awake
to Reality—about being fully human.

In many ways this book reflects the words and actions of
Gautama Siddhartha, known more commonly as the Buddha
("one who has awakened"). This book, however, is not an ex-
ploration of what the Buddha said and did; rather, it explores
what the world reveals to all of us, right now, in *this moment*.

In his talks and dialogues, the Buddha was only pointing out what he saw and experienced directly. This book is based on the fact that this same vision and experience are available to all of us, without exception, right now.

The Buddha was not interested in theology or cosmology. He didn't speak on these subjects and in fact would not answer questions on them. His primary concerns were psychological, moral, and highly practical ones:

- How can we *see* the world as it comes to be in each moment rather than as what we think, hope, or fear it is?

- How can we base our actions on Reality rather than on the longing and loathing of our hearts and minds?

- How can we live lives that are wise, compassionate, and in tune with Reality?

- What is the experience of being awake?

Can there be any questions about life that are more practical, down-to-earth, and immediately relevant than these?

After he responded to such questions, however, the Buddha asked people not to mindlessly accept his words but to investigate for themselves the immediate experience of Mind. "Be a light unto yourselves," he told his listeners. "Don't look for refuge to anyone besides yourselves." Over and over, he urged people: "Purify your own minds."

Yet the Buddha wasn't talking about wiping our minds clean of foul thoughts or inclinations. Such efforts can easily turn into a denial of our humanity—and, anyway, they don't work. Actively trying to purge ourselves of unwholesome thoughts only cuts us off and sets us apart from others. Soon we develop notions of how we're superior to those who don't follow our way. Such an approach itself gives off a foul odor. How can we purify our minds in this way when the very impulse to do so is already born of impurity?

In saying "purify your own minds," the Buddha was pointing to something very different. That "something very different" is the subject of this book: waking up.

This is why the Buddha urged people not to blindly follow traditions, reports, hearsay, opinions, speculation, or the authority of religious texts but to *see* and *know* for ourselves what is True—and, when we do, to take it up. He also urged us to *see* and *know* for ourselves what is hurtful and divisive—and to give that up. The emphasis is always on *seeing* and *knowing*, not on thinking, calculating, and believing.

Two points should be mentioned here. First, as we will see, what we call "mind" turns out to be vastly more than the thoughts, images, emotions, explanations, and questions we think our brains churn out. In fact, there is another aspect of mind that is boundless and not limited to our personal experiences of thought and thing, yet it's completely accessible in every moment.

Second, certain themes necessarily emerge and reemerge as we investigate the subject of mind: attention, intention, honesty with oneself, wisdom, true compassion, and the pure, genuine, undiluted desire to wake up. These themes will intertwine more or less continuously throughout this book's forty-three chapters.

This book is organized in three sections. In part 1 we look at our confusion. Generally, for us, the world is muddy water. We don't *know* what's going on. We think we do, of course, much of the time. But when we look carefully, as we do in part 1, we can see a great deal of confusion within many of our common, unquestioned, everyday views of the world.

In part 2 we look again at our experience but now with a view that is less bound by our common assumptions, which are the source of virtually all of our confusion.

Finally, in part 3, we become aware that direct experience is the pure experience of Mind itself, yet it is not at all what we think.

This book focuses on the common yet generally unheeded confusion that underlies virtually all of the moment-by-moment questions and choices we face. It does not, how-ever—and cannot—provide answers and correct options for you. Instead, it can help you do something far more valuable: recognize the inappropriateness, and the futility, of how we usually approach life's most troubling issues. More valuable still, it can help us fully know lives of joy and freedom through the practice of pure awareness. In short, it can help us wake up and *see* Reality for ourselves.

Steve Hagen
Dharma Field Meditation
and Learning Center
Minneapolis, Minnesota
April 2003

*Those who do not understand the distinctions
between the two truths (relative and
Absolute) do not understand the profound truth
embodied in the Buddha's message.*

—Nagarjuna

When we see a relative truth—as in "I see the book before me"—we employ the conventional use of the term "to see." The *seeing* of ultimate Reality, however, is quite another matter. When such objectless Awareness—*seeing, knowing,* etc.—is referred to in this book, the word will be italicized. This should not be mistaken for merely emphasizing those words.

Similarly, initial capital letters will be used in words that reflect the Absolute aspect of experience—i.e., Truth, Awareness, Reality, etc.

PART ONE

MUDDY WATER

PART FOUR

MUDDY WATER

PARADOX AND CONFUSION

I F Y O U V I S I T a Buddhist temple in Japan, you'll likely encounter two gigantic, fierce, demonlike figures standing at either side of the entrance. These are called the guardians of Truth, and their names are Paradox and Confusion.

When I first encountered these figures, it had never occurred to me that Truth had guards—or, indeed, that it needed guarding. But if the notion had arisen in my mind, I suspect I would have pictured very pleasing, angelic figures.

Why were these creatures so terrifying and menacing? And why were the *guardians* of Truth represented rather than Truth itself?

Gradually, I began to see the implication. There can be no image of Truth. Truth can't be captured in an image or a phrase or a word. It can't be laid out in a theory, a diagram, or a book. Whatever notions we might have about Truth are incapable of bringing us to it. Thus, in trying to take hold of Truth, we naturally encounter paradox and confusion.

It works like this: though we experience Reality directly, we ignore it. Instead, we try to explain it or take hold of it through ideas, models, beliefs, and stories. But precisely because these things *aren't* Reality, our explanations naturally never match actual experience. In the disjoint between Reality and our explanations of it, paradox and confusion naturally arise.

Furthermore, any accurate statement we would make about Truth must contain within itself its own demise. Thus such a statement inevitably will appear paradoxical and contradictory. In other words, statements about Truth and Reality are not like ordinary statements.

Usually we make a statement to single something out, to pin something down and make it unambiguous. Not so if our business is Truth. In this case we must be willing to encounter, rather than try to evade, paradox and confusion.

Our problem with paradox and confusion is that we insist on putting our direct experience into a conceptual box. We try to encapsulate our experience in frozen, changeless form: "this means that."

Ordinary statements don't permit paradox. Rather, they try to pin down their subjects and make them appear as real and solid as possible. Ordinary statements are presented in the spirit of "This is the Truth; believe it." Then we're handed something, often in the form of a book or a pamphlet.

But all statements that present themselves in this way— whether they're about politics, morality, economics, psychology, religion, science, philosophy, mathematics, or auto mechanics—

are just ordinary stuff. They're not Truth; they're merely the attempt to preserve what necessarily passes away.

When we claim to describe what's Really going on by our words, no matter how beautiful, such words are already in error. Truth simply can't be re-presented.

We want Truth badly. We want to hold it tightly in our hand. We want to give it to others in a word or a phrase. We want something we can jot down. Something we can impress upon others—and impress others with.

We act as though Truth were something we could stuff in our pockets, something we could take out every once in a while to show people, saying, "Here, this is it!" We forget that they will show us *their* slips of paper, with other ostensible Truths written upon them.

But Truth is not like this. Indeed, how could it be?

We need only *see* that it's beyond the spin of paradox that Truth and Reality are glimpsed. If we would simply not try to pin Reality down, confusion would no longer turn us away.

What we can do is carefully attend to what's actually going on around us—and notice that our formulated beliefs, concepts, and stories never fully explain what's going on.

Our eyes must remain open long enough that we may be suddenly overwhelmed by a new experience—a new awareness—that shatters our habitual thought and our old familiar stories.

We can free ourselves from paradox and confusion only when we set ourselves in an open and inquiring frame of mind while ever on guard that we do not insist upon some particular belief, no matter how seemingly well justified.

If it's Truth we're after, we'll find that we cannot start with *any* assumptions or concepts whatsoever. Instead, we must approach the world with bare, naked attention, *seeing* it without any mental bias—without concepts, beliefs, preconceptions, presumptions, or expectations.

Doing this is the subject of this book.

2

STEPPING ON REALITY

THE FIVE PRECEPTS, listed here, are generally recognized by most Buddhists, though they're expressed in a variety of forms. They're not commandments but descriptions of the moral stance that would necessarily be taken by one who is on the path to Awakening.

1. A follower of the Way does not kill.

2. A follower of the Way does not take what is not given.

3. A follower of the Way does not abuse the senses.

4. A follower of the Way does not speak deceptively.

5. A follower of the Way does not intoxicate oneself or others.

There are additional precepts in Buddhism as well. In all cases, however, if we are to think, speak, and act as moral agents, what we do must come out of wisdom and compassion—from *seeing*—and not from some structure imposed upon us.

There's a Zen story about a student who made a special point of keeping all the Buddhist precepts. Once, however, while walking at night, he stepped on something that made a squishing sound. He imagined that he must have stepped on an egg-bearing frog. Immediately he was filled with fear and regret, for the precepts include not killing. When he went to sleep that night he dreamed that hundreds of frogs came to him, demanding his life in exchange.

When morning came, he went back to the place the incident had occurred and found that he had stepped on an overripe eggplant. Suddenly his confusion stopped.

From that moment on, the story says, he knew how to practice Zen and how to truly follow the precepts.

Like many people who practice Buddhism sincerely, this student erroneously thought of the precepts as a training manual or code of behavior. Identifying himself as someone who had mastered this training and who could keep the precepts, he created all kinds of trouble for himself and for others. Although he could expound upon the precepts at length, when he stepped on something squishy in the night, his understanding of the precepts did nothing to bring him peace or stability of mind. In fact, it did just the opposite: he needlessly tortured himself with guilt.

The student's problem was that he thought he understood something that he didn't. He thought he had stepped on and killed a frog, but he hadn't. He also thought that he understood the precepts, but he was wrong here, too. In both cases, rather than honestly admitting and facing what he didn't know, he imagined he did know.

Because he had only an intellectual understanding of the precept against taking life, he was thrown into anguish. He had completely forgotten that in Reality he didn't know what he stepped on. And instead of living with that uncertainty, he made up an explanation for what happened—and made himself miserable believing it.

This story reminds us that if you hold the precepts in your mind, then you don't understand them, for the precepts are not anything you can grasp or package up into concepts.

To keep the Buddhist precepts, we simply must be *here*, immediately present with what's going on and not lost in thought or speculation. We need to *see* what's going on in *this moment*—including what's going on in our own mind.

And when we don't know what's going on—when, for example, we step on something in the dark—then it means fully realizing that we don't know. This is the deeper understanding of this story—to *know* when you don't know.

We often think we *know* things when in fact it's only our imagination taking us further and further away from what is actually happening. What we imagine then seems very real to us. Soon we're caught up in our imaginary longings and loathings.

But if you're *here*—truly present—you realize there's nothing to run from or to go after. You can stay calm, even if you did accidentally step on a frog. Just be with *this moment* and *see* what's going on. Know your own mind.

This story is about how we conjure up imaginary worlds and trap ourselves in them. But if we would only look carefully, we would *see* that the world is not the way we think it is—and that it can never be the way we think it is.

We strive to master and control our imaginary worlds. We create all kinds of rules and regulations, goals and values, do's and don'ts, and we strive to become skilled in dealing with them all. This is where we expend so much of our time and energy yet exercise so little of our awareness.

What the Buddhist precepts are about is noticing how we do these things all the time. The precepts direct us to notice what's going on from moment to moment—to *see* what's going on in your mind right *now*. How does it lean—toward this or away from that?

The precepts help us to come back to *this moment*—where Reality is immediately experienced—before we interpret anything.

Moment after moment, we have to come back to *this moment* to *see* what is actually taking place. Otherwise we live in a fantasy world where we see ourselves as separate and where we become preoccupied with pleasing and protecting ourselves.

When the student in this story saw the squashed eggplant, he suddenly woke up—not just to the reality of what he had stepped on, but to how he had been creating all kinds of needless and distracting fears and concepts in his mind. He suddenly *saw* the imaginary worlds he'd been creating for himself, and he woke from his dream of separation, pride, and guilt.

In just such a moment—at the sight of a squashed fruit, at the sound of a pebble striking wood, at the sight of the morning star—any of us can awaken. Nothing holds us back but our thought.

3

THE PROBLEM
WITH ERADICATING EVIL

But I say unto you, that ye resist not evil. . . .

—Jesus of Nazareth

MATTHEW 5:39

SOME YEARS AGO I came upon a beautiful picture: the original image of the three famous monkeys, Hear No Evil, Speak No Evil, See No Evil. They were carved into the lintel of a stable door in seventeenth-century Japan.

As a boy, I remember seeing plaster images of these three, but they didn't look at all like the monkeys of old Japan. The figurines I knew were tame by comparison, with all three lethargically squatting and facing the same direction. As originally carved in Japan, however, they were quite dynamic and captivating. All were active, striking out in different directions. Rather than refusing to acknowledge evil, as the more familiar image seems to depict, these monkeys appeared to be scrambling in response to it.

We tend to think of evil as something distinct and separate—especially separate from us, the good folks. And we're preoccupied with keeping it that way. As a result, we often view certain people or cultures or political systems or religions as evil. Indeed, we can decide that just about anything is evil. (I remember once being told that Lake Superior was evil because it has taken the lives of so many people.)

But any belief that evil is (or could ever be) separate from us leaves us struggling to keep evil ever at bay.

We see ourselves as divided and separated from experience. We see ourselves as experiencers of "that, out there." And when that, out there, seems to please or protect us, we call it good. Similarly, when it appears threatening or strange or terrifying, we call it evil. Thus our feeling of separateness is precisely what creates notions of good and evil in the first place.

Were we to *see* the world as it is, however, thoughts of good and evil simply would not arise.

Consider the utter foolishness with which we repeat (and feed) the cycle. First we imagine complete separateness, then we react emotionally to what we imagine. Then, based on our emotional responses—we fear this, we want that—we imagine mental objects that we call good and evil. But they're not real, as we imagine. They're phantoms we've created in response to other phantoms.

This problem has a more profound aspect. In our desperation to create and maintain our separateness from evil—in our futile attempts to do the impossible—we create all kinds of problems for ourselves and others. These problems in turn also get branded as evil. Sometimes we get branded as evil as well. And so the chain goes on and on. We would rather call down war upon ourselves and others, wallowing in and grasping at our conceptual distinctions, than notice the ungraspable world of Wholeness and Totality that we're already immersed in.

The fact is that we're always in (and part of) Totality. We cannot remove ourselves or anything else—any thought, any thing—from it.

If we were to *see* this, we'd have a completely different take on this matter of good and evil, one that would cease to embroil us in pain and confusion.

This is not to say that we don't experience things that are painful or sorrowful or difficult. But the awakened mind, which *sees* all experience as a Whole, doesn't see evil as such. It doesn't interpret experience as "something out there that threatens me." By the same token, it doesn't see good "out there" either, as something apart and separate.

In awakening to our experience as a Whole, we realize that it's this kind of thinking itself that is the problem. Here is the root of all our sorrow, pain, suffering, and confusion.

According to the Buddhadharma (the teaching of the Awakened), our effort is to live fully and compassionately in this world of muddy water without churning it up all the more. To do this, we only need to realize that whatever comes our way is already of the Whole and cannot be done away with. We need to take care of it on *this* ground where we find ourselves.

This is not to condone whatever brutality, rage, vengefulness, or destructiveness may arise. If there's confusion, maybe we can shed a little light. If there's pain, perhaps we can do something to ease it. If there's violence, it may be possible to absorb it—while also doing what can be done to reduce it.

The first thing *you* need to do, however, is observe your own mind.

We need to *see* that we're not—and never were and never will be—separate or removed from others. We need to look at our own minds honestly and dispassionately, noticing how they lean toward and away from the innumerable distractions and concepts they imagine.

This is why, in the *Dhammapada*, the Buddha gives us the admonition to purify our own minds. It's the last place we may want to look, but it's only *here* that we can live freely in the world without seeing others, or ourselves, as evil.

Our very quickness to express things in terms of good and evil is what creates divisiveness and human misery. When we *see* this, we can begin to act wisely.

When we catch ourselves adrift in our divisive thoughts, or when we get caught up in our judgments about "them" (or "us"), we can bring ourselves back to *this*. All we need is a little bit of attention, a little bit of reflection, and a little bit of patience.

See confusion as confusion. Acknowledge suffering as suffering. Feel pain and sorrow and divisiveness. Experience anger or fear or shock for what they are. But you don't have to think of them as evil—as intrinsically bad, as needing to be destroyed or driven from our midst. On the contrary, they need to be absorbed, healed, made whole.

Like ourselves, whatever we may want to call evil is already a part of the Whole and cannot be removed. To *see* in this way is to purify your own mind.

4

WE'VE GOT IT ALL
BACKWARD

MANY PEOPLE put religion and science in separate, hermetically sealed boxes. Most of us, however, don't realize that many aspects of religion and science were conjoined for many centuries before we put them into these boxes. In fact, at one time, before science really came into its own, science and religion were one and the same.

This isn't really so strange when we note that their common origin lies in our deep desire to *know*, to *realize* Truth.

Consider, for example, what religion is actually about. The word *religion* came from *religio*, which meant "to bind back or very strongly to Truth." Thus the heart of religion is about *seeing* or experiencing Truth—not about holding a set of beliefs. *Religio* comes out of our deeply felt desire to get back to Truth. We don't want to be deceived.

Like religion, science is also about getting to Truth. The term *science* comes from the Latin *scire*, "to know." Science, as

I've often heard it said by scientists themselves, is about knowing, not about believing.

But the place we tend not to look—the place we really get it backward, the place we really go wrong—is this area of belief. Indeed, as we commonly think of science and religion, each claims an attribute that more naturally (and properly) belongs to the other. While religion is commonly thought to be about belief, its natural concern is actually with Knowledge, with *knowing*. And while science is thought to be about actual Knowledge, and fancies itself to be independent of belief, it is in fact inherently quite dependent upon it.

An article appeared not too long ago in the *New York Times* entitled "Crossing Flaming Swords over God and Physics." It was about a debate between Steven Weinberg, the Nobel laureate in physics, and John Polkinghorne, a knighted physicist and Anglican priest. It was presented as a match between the "believer" (Polkinghorne) and the "nonbeliever" (Weinberg). But, in fact, that's not what it was at all. Their interaction, as described in the article, almost "deteriorate[d] into a physical fight."

If Dr. Weinberg had been genuinely a nonbeliever, there would have been no problem. In fact, this event was not a debate between a nonbeliever and a believer but a confrontation between two ardent believers. It was a standoff between two men who believed two very different views.

The real issue is not science versus religion or even belief versus nonbelief. The most angry and virulent debates in the world (and the worst violent clashes) are inevitably between one believer and another. Once two headstrong believers spar off, the odds of coming to any amicable resolution are nil.

The fact is that science needs belief. It can't function without it. Science requires that we construct conceptualized versions of the world. It needs us to break the world apart so that we can examine it. This isn't wrong; indeed, there's great value in it. In this sense, then, science makes *greater* use of belief and is more dependent upon it than is religion.

In contrast, for religion to function properly—that is, for it to help us open our eyes to Truth—it *shouldn't* require belief. After all, religion is fundamentally about direct Knowledge of Truth. Thus, all religion needs to require of people is an earnest desire to *know*, to *see*, to wake up. This is enough.

Unfortunately, in practice, religion makes wide use of beliefs—beliefs about how we got here, what our purpose is, where we're going, and so forth—all in a desperate attempt to make sense of the world and our experience in it. As Joseph Campbell put it, religion short-circuits the religious experience by putting it into concepts.

But for religion to continue to function at its best, it would do well to get out of this business of belief entirely, to stop forming inevitably inaccurate conceptual models of Reality. This has become more properly the territory of science, not religion.

In short, science is well positioned to properly handle belief. Religion is not.

Science goes to great lengths to test its beliefs (which it calls hypotheses), to verify or disprove their validity. Science tests its hypotheses, and if they're in error they're thrown out or reformulated and tested again. Tests must then be replicated many times by others. It's an impeccable method for arriving at truth—that is, relative, practical, everyday truth.

Science, however, can reveal to us nothing at all about ultimate Truth. This is, instead, the legitimate province—and responsibility—of religion.

Using the scientific method, we can clear up a lot of misconceptions about the nature of the relative world—the world of this and that—and about how things function and interact. But there's nothing about this method that finally brings us to understand, directly and immediately, what's actually going on. This belongs to religion—but only so long as religion doesn't wallow in belief.

Religion is not equipped to test and verify hypotheses. Nor should it be. It doesn't need the scientific method *because it needn't and shouldn't make use of hypotheses* or rely on beliefs of any kind.

Unfortunately, because all religions, including Buddhism, *do* indulge in beliefs, everyone goes running off in different directions, carrying their separate banners of belief, signifying nothing but human delusion and folly. As a result, we have religions fighting each other and religions fighting science. As my teacher, Jikai Dainin Katagiri, used to say, "Under the beautiful flag of religion, we fight."

But it's not religion that creates this situation. It's the fact that we're constantly reaching for something we can grab hold of. We want to say, "Ah, this is it. This is how it is. This is the Truth; believe it!"

But to the extent that we do this, we do not (and cannot) arrive at Truth because Truth—ultimate Reality—is not something we *can* believe. That is, it isn't something we can formulate in a concept of any kind.

At some point we have to settle into realizing what the deep need of the human heart really is: we want to get back to Truth. This feeling is often innocently yet eloquently expressed in religion. It's pure heart and mind, yet with no specific point or agenda. And when we quiet our busy minds, this purity of heart and mind can be immediately felt.

But, instead, we habitually look to something outside our selves, something "out there" in the world—or even "out there" *beyond* the world—that will save us, something that will serve as a go-between.

This all comes out of our confusion and out of the fear that we're somehow removed from Truth, that there's some innate separation in the first place.

But there isn't. And what we most need to do as human beings—and what religion, in its purest form, can help us do— is quiet down and realize this.

. . .

Shunryu Suzuki wrote in his first book, *Zen Mind, Beginner's Mind,*

> *I have discovered that it is necessary, absolutely necessary,
> to believe in nothing. That is, we have to believe in some-
> thing which has no form and no color—something which
> exists before all forms and colors appear. This is a very
> important point.*

Or, as the ninth-century Chinese Zen teacher Huang Po put it, "The foolish reject what they *see,* not what they think; the wise reject what they think, not what they *see.*"

Instead of putting faith in what we believe, think, explain, justify, or otherwise construct in our minds, we can learn to put our trust and confidence in immediate, direct experience, before all forms and colors appear. Religion, in its most essential expression, can help us do this.

This is faith in its purest form: trust in actual experience before we make anything of it—before beliefs, thoughts, signs, explanations, justifications, and other constructions of our minds take form.

This is the great sanity, the great compassion, the great wisdom that religion holds for us. This sanity, compassion, and wisdom all come out of simply learning to trust that Truth is right at hand. There's no go-between. You don't get it from a teacher, from an institution, or from a belief system of any sort. You don't get it from a book, either. Indeed, you can't.

In fact, you don't get it from anything. You don't need to get it. You already have it. You're inseparable from it. You only need to *just see*.

Whether we're religious or not, in holding to beliefs and identifying with them, in shutting down and closing ourselves off from others, in this and so many other ways we create the most urgent and penetrating problems for ourselves.

We're all human. We all have the desire to awaken, though we may not all be so aware. And we can all be moved by the human condition.

But without taking hold of any thought or thing, just realize what's *seen* directly, before you make anything of it. This is to *know* Truth. It has nothing to do with belief.

5

THE ITCH IN YOUR MIND

OFTEN, WHEN WE'RE caught up in our dualistic thinking, we say to ourselves, "I'm deluded, so I want to become enlightened." Yet we don't realize that we're already immersed in enlightenment.

We sit here, thinking that there's something else, something better, over there—something we need to get, attain, or accomplish. Then we take up meditation with the idea that this practice will somehow lead us to enlightenment.

We think this—in fact, we believe it fervently—even though we're told over and over and over again, through all kinds of examples and stories, that this is not the way Reality works.

We hear about Baso, who meditated to become a buddha until his teacher started polishing a tile to, as he put it, "turn it into a mirror." Baso got the message: just as no amount of polishing will turn a tile into a mirror, no amount of meditating will turn you into a buddha. How could it? You're already Buddha—that is, inseparable from Reality and Truth. Yet we ignore this and carry on as though we're all missing or lacking something.

Suzuki Roshi tells us in *Zen Mind, Beginner's Mind* that there's no gaining idea in Zen practice. If there is, it's not practice. We're told this over and over and over and over and over and *over* again. For years we are told this; if we study with a true teacher, we'll get a full dose of it.

Yet in our minds, we let the basic delusion go on. We indulge and delight in it. We keep hoping that somehow we'll throw the right spiritual switch and enlightenment will flash on at last.

Can we, with sheer and simple honesty, look at this little festering idea in our minds? We need to do this. We have to take this to heart. We have to be serious about it.

Once we admit this idea is there, what are we going to do about it? Drive it out? Pretend it's not there? "I'm not really doing this because I want to be enlightened. I'm doing it just to do it. I'm sure I have no ulterior motives at all." If it's there, you have to acknowledge it. There's no point in denying it or fighting it or thinking, "I shouldn't be this way." Why *shouldn't* you be that way? It's very normal for you to be that way. It's nothing to be ashamed of. In fact, if you start getting down on yourself for desiring enlightenment, you'll just keep on feeding that desire. You're going to keep creating the same problem over and over in one form or another.

Indeed, all you have to do is recognize what's going on in your mind. Then, and *only* then, can you begin to realize that you'll never be free as long as you hang on to either the desire for enlightenment or the desire to get beyond a desire for enlightenment.

This is a point you have to become very clear on. It's when you thoroughly understand this, and not before, that your festering mind, of itself, drops off. Then you truly begin to practice Zen.

We have to realize thoroughly the nature of our grasping minds. Zen is never a matter of adding something to your mind or removing something from it or denying how it functions. These things don't work because they have nothing to do with Reality. If grasping *is* your mind in this moment, then this is your mind. This is simply how it is; there's no point in pretending otherwise. Let's be honest.

Here's another way of looking at it.

Do you really think that there's something you can put in your mind, or take out of it, that's going to satisfy the deep ache of the heart? "I want to be awake." "I want enlightenment." "I want understanding." "I want freedom and peace of mind." It's like an itch in your mind, yet you're left with no hand to scratch it with.

Do you really think that there's something "out there"— enlightenment, Nirvana, some special insight—that's ever going to satisfy? Have you ever known *anything* to truly satisfy the existential itch in your mind? Nothing ever has. Nothing ever will. Momentarily you may satisfy it, but even if you do, notice that "over there," there's just one more thing. As long as you hold yourself apart, there's always something you have to get or get away from. The supply of such things is endless. Thus we make enlightenment into just another urge, another itch we try to scratch.

What you are truly after neither has form nor is without form. It cannot be grasped or attained or obtained or conceptualized or even described.

So what *can* we do?

We can understand the nature of our situation. We can realize that our life can't be separated from Reality—from the life of the world as a Whole, from the lives of others. In other words, there's nothing to get.

In practical terms, it means we can notice—and root out by simply noticing—the grasping of our own minds as we live from day to day. We can realize, right up front, that this very restless, itching mind that asks, "What am I getting out of this?" and "What's best for me?" is already the pain and the confusion we wish to free ourselves from.

6

A MIND OF WINTER

IN THE STORY "The Sorcerer's Apprentice," the apprentice must attend to many mundane chores. But he doesn't have much love for menial work. Instead, he wants power. He wants to be like his master and not have to trouble himself with mundane matters.

Since he has learned a few tricks from the master, he decides to use them to make his work easier. He knows a spell he can cast on the broom to make it do his bidding, like drawing water from the well for the master's bath.

The problem, however, is that the apprentice doesn't know everything he needs to know to wield such power properly. He is able to get the broom to sprout hands, pick up buckets, and haul water, but when it comes time to tell the broom to stop, the apprentice doesn't know the right command. And now the tub is overflowing, but the broom just keeps adding more water to it.

The apprentice pleads with the broom, but the broom tells him, "I can't stop; you must give me the correct command." The apprentice has unleashed something in the world that he doesn't know how to undo.

In desperation he takes hold of an ax and swings at the broom, cutting it in two. Momentarily it works. The fragments of the broom fall to the floor. But soon each half sprouts its missing half so that each part has now turned into a full broom, and each broom has two hands. Both brooms pick up buckets and continue to haul water, which now begins to flood the room.

This is both a desperate story and, in many ways, a familiar one. Once we've started on a path, we often discover that we haven't the capacity to save ourselves or stop. We've acquired too much power, more than we can handle. We want to use it, but we can't control ourselves. We're too impulsive. We act before we see.

For example, take nanotechnology, the technology of the very small, which enables us to make machines on a molecular scale. We are learning to build microscopic machines and robots, some of which will have the ability to reproduce themselves. While we might be able to get such little devices to do all kinds of nifty things for us, we might also discover that we've created something we'd later like to stop—and find that we have no way to do so.

Imagine billions of tiny machines with the ability to replicate themselves from materials in the environment. If such devices ever got loose, particularly if they had the ability to modify themselves, how could we maintain control over them? They might become like viruses but with no antibodies to stop them. Bill Joy, the head scientist at Sun Microsystems, became alarmed when he realized that this kind of technology is on the horizon and potentially accessible not just to the scientists at Bell Labs, but to anyone with a home computer.

Stories such as "The Sorcerer's Apprentice" and Bill Joy's nightmarish forecast are archetypal. They come out of a deep suspicion we have about our desire for control and the limits of our ability to control our own impulses. The various Faust stories get at this, as do *Frankenstein* and *The Strange Case of Dr. Jekyll and Mr. Hyde*.

Zen literature has such a story as well. In it a fellow comes upon a demon for sale at a carnival—and very cheap, too. "What can it do?" he asks. "This demon will do anything for you," the merchant tells him. "Just tell it what you want done, and it will do it. It will do your laundry, cook your meals, do your shopping. It will handle all your chores around the house. The only thing to remember is that you must keep it busy."

The man, focused on his immediate concerns, thinks this is a bargain. He buys it and takes it home.

At first all is well. Just as promised, the demon quickly goes to work, taking care of whatever the man commands it to do. The demon fixes the roof, cooks meals, and plants the garden. Of course, the man has to keep coming up with things for the demon to do. Yet this still seems doable—until, one day, the man has to step away briefly on personal business. When he returns only a short while later, the demon is roasting the neighbor's child on a spit.

We are foolish to think we can have mastery over what is not ours to master.

All of us look for things that will make life easier for ourselves. We think, "Wouldn't it be great if I could create this or do that or avoid those?" Yet we overlook the larger ramifications that come with everything we do. We look at everything in terms of ourselves, with rarely a thought for what lies beyond our immediate circumstances.

The crux of all these stories, and our basic problem, is our preoccupation with pleasing and protecting ourselves. In the process of trying to attain security, we make ourselves insecure. To the extent that we want knowledge, we perplex and baffle ourselves. And to the extent that we want power, we undermine our ability to wield power wisely. Whenever we're driven by ego, we net the opposite (or the converse) of what we go after.

The question is: Is another kind of mind possible?

Consider the mind of a man named Han-shan, who lived during the T'ang period in China and who is a very popular figure in Zen literature. In Chinese his name means "cold mountain." According to custom, he took this name from the place where he lived, which is in the T'ien T'ai range in China. He lived near a monastery, Kuo-ch'ing, which he frequented.

Han-shan became good friends with Shih-te, the head of the dining hall at Kuo-ch'ing. (Shih-te is often depicted holding a broom. Clearly, he didn't have the sorcerer's apprentice's desire that the broom should do his work for him.) Han-shan and Shih-te are often described as the two Zen fools, and they are pictured laughing and delighting in the most ordinary things—like a leaf falling from a tree.

Han-shan was a free spirit. He didn't care what people thought of him. And many thought he was a fool because he was dirty, disheveled, and poor. Yet none of this was of any concern to him. Even though Han-shan wasn't a monk, the abbot of the monastery said that he had more wisdom than most of the monks who were training there.

Sometimes, when he'd leave Kuo-ch'ing to return to Cold Mountain, monks would chase after him, making fun of him and his foolish antics. But Han-shan would laugh right along with them. Then he'd continue on his way.

Han-shan would write poems and leave them on trees, on rocks, on walls. Eventually, someone collected a number of them, luckily for us. Over three hundred of them were gathered in all. They show us a very different kind of mind than the ego-driven mind most of us are so familiar with.

Cold Mountain wrote:

People ask the way to Cold Mountain.
There's no trail.

Even in summer, ice doesn't melt.
Rolling fog obscures the rising sun.

How did I get here?
My heart's not like yours.
If your heart was like mine,
You'd be here.

Whenever I see people, I only say,
"Aim for Cold Mountain."

When people first encounter Zen, they're often intrigued by Han-shan. They want to know the way to Cold Mountain. They ask, "How can I be like that? How can my mind be as free as his?"

But, as Han-shan answered, "There's no trail." There can't be. There's no way *here*.

We don't even understand what we're asking when we ask this question. We think we're asking for freedom, but we're really asking for something outside ourselves—something we can take hold of, something we can control and use to arrange our comfort. And we think that Han-shan, or Zen, will provide us with a map to guide us there.

Han-shan didn't play this game. He didn't need to. You don't need to, either. You're already *here*. We're always *here*. In fact, you can't leave.

We think we have to get this, get away from that. We think we can have power over this, can control that. Above all, we think that the mind of Cold Mountain is inaccessible to people like us. But in this, we're dead wrong.

Consider the twentieth-century writer Wallace Stevens, who alludes to such a mind in his poem "The Snow Man":

One must have a mind of winter
To regard the frost and the boughs
Of the pinetrees crusted with snow;

And have been cold a long time
To behold the junipers shagged with ice,
The spruces rough in the distant glitter

Of the January sun; and not to think
Of any misery in the sound of the wind,
In the sound of a few leaves,

Which is the sound of the land
Full of the same wind
That is blowing in the same bare place

For the listener, who listens in the snow,
And, nothing himself, beholds
Nothing that is not there and the nothing that is.

Like Han-shan, Wallace Stevens was not a monk (in fact, he was a wealthy businessman), yet he understood this mind of Totality—this mind that includes everything.

Zen is about *knowing* this mind, which can only be found and expressed right *here*.

There's no trail to this place. We're already *here*. All of us. If it's winter, one must have a mind of winter—indeed, one must *be* winter—to be *here*. That is, not thinking of spring, not longing for summer, for something that doesn't exist *now*, *here*. *This* mind isn't reaching for some other place.

And if it's summer, one must have a mind of summer.

There *is* no other place. We're forever *here*.

We don't need to control the world. We don't need to defend ourselves against it. We don't need to preserve anything. We only need to be *here*—totally, completely, freely—responding to the actual occasion.

If we were truly *here*, we'd behold nothing that is not *here*. We'd not be taken in by the illusion of self and by all the fuss that's required for its pleasure and protection.

Truth cannot be something else or somewhere else. There cannot be models of it. It cannot be diagrammed or written out. It cannot be held as a possession of mind. And how kind of Han-shan to point all this out.

There's only this one place: *right here, right now.* This is why Han-shan said, "If your heart was like mine, you'd be here." To be *here* is freedom from insanity, fear, worry, struggle, striving, the urgent desire to control, and the habitual yearning for security and escape from pain.

When Han-shan writes, "Whenever I see people, I only say, 'aim for Cold Mountain,'" this is his invitation to each of us just to be *here*. To awaken to your own crazy mind, your own grasping heart.

This is to make it to Cold Mountain.

7

NO MYSTERY

T HERE'S NO MYSTERY to life. We just think there is.

The mystery is something we make up, something we construct in our minds.

We do this in much the same way that we construct ideas about God or Truth or Reality or Buddha or goodness—or anything, really. And we construct them without even realizing that we do it.

Mystery appears anytime we create a mental form. For example, we attribute all kinds of qualities to our created notion of God. "God is good." And God has intention. "He has a plan for me." And God is a he or a she. When we do this, sooner or later we'll get to the point where we have to declare God a mystery. "God moves in mysterious ways."

In the same way, we may have notions about good and evil, about heaven and hell, about angels and devils. And they're all cloaked and woven in mystery simply because we've conceptualized them. We've made them up.

William Shakespeare, in a beautiful and oft-quoted line from *The Tempest*, wrote, "We are such stuff as dreams are made on, and our little life is rounded with a sleep." In this line he speaks to us much like the awakened would. Often in Buddhist literature we find similar references to the realization that life is like a dream, like a fantasy.

The awakened *see* this. In fact, they're called awakened precisely because enlightenment is like waking from a dream. Our common, everyday reality is dreamlike, but we don't recognize it. We don't *see* that it's a constructed reality—pure mental fabrication.

If we're in bed dreaming and then we wake up, the vivid experience we had only moments before—the colors, the sounds, the smells, the feelings—are all still with us but fading fast. We say, "It was only a dream."

Only a dream . . . but now what? Now "I am awake. This is reality. Here I am." But to the awakened this is still a dream, still mental fabrication. It isn't full awareness.

We don't know what's going on. We don't understand what human life is all about. We don't understand the "big question." We're not even sure what that question is.

What's existence all about? How did I get here? Where am I going? Why is there something as opposed to nothing? When we ponder these questions, the world can seem mysterious and dreamlike indeed.

If we simply look around ourselves, the same qualities of mystery and unreality appear. In the first twenty or thirty feet around us, everything seems distinct—clear and bright. But the moment we venture further, things start to dim. As we look into the outer reaches around us, we don't see anything at all. We don't understand human life; we don't seem to understand what anything is.

As we gaze into our own past, the same thing happens: our own lives fade and dim. We might have vivid memories, but they're all of a world that doesn't exist now.

The future is no different. We can speculate and wonder, dream and anticipate, or become filled with dread and fear, but it's all still a mystery.

Darkness seems to completely surround us, both in time and space. Not just figuratively but literally. As we look into the night sky, we seem to be surrounded by blackness.

So here we are, living this dreamlike existence. The moment we step away from the bright circle of our immediate concerns—our immediate surroundings, our preoccupation of the moment—everything becomes dim and dark.

But to those who are awake, Reality is just the opposite. The only mysteries are in the details of our immediate concerns: we're not sure why the computer won't work or what made that thumping sound in the garage or what happened to that book we enjoyed so much—we always placed it on this particular shelf, in this particular spot. These small fragments of darkness are always close at hand.

But to the awakened, what surrounds this darkness—and us—is light. There's no mystery. Reality is clear, obvious, and (metaphorically) well illumined.

If you pay careful attention to your actual experience, this is what you'll find. There's truly no ultimate mystery at all, until we grasp.

The Buddha said, "Be a light unto yourself; betake yourselves to no external refuge." Why? Because there *is* no such refuge. Nor is any needed. *The thing you want to reach for to sustain you and help you is merely a construct of your own imagination.* Ultimately, it will only hinder you, perpetuating your feeling of vulnerability.

It's better instead to *just look* at the situation you're in and *see* immediately and directly what's going on. If you do this honestly and earnestly, you'll see that you're already sustained, complete, and whole and that everything you'll ever truly need is at hand.

When we see ourselves as a little self, we don't realize that we're caught up in our thinking. It's all just mental construction, and what goes along with it is the deep desire to protect the imagined thing we call "me." We don't realize how profoundly uncomfortable we make ourselves by interpreting our experience in this way. We become preoccupied with trying to protect this little self from the deep mystery we've created around it as well as with trying to please it. What we rarely seem to notice is that it won't stay pleased.

There's a poem by Jacque Prévert that sums up this basic confusion quite well. He wrote:

I am what I am
I was made like this
What more do you want
What do you want of me

"I was made like this." Made like what? Nothing holds still. We can *see* this.

"What do you want of me?" What everyone expects of you (and what you ought to expect of yourself if you want to be happy rather than plagued by this imaginary thing you think you need to please and protect) is that you be a buddha—that is, awake.

And what is Buddha? Reality. All of it. The Whole. Nothing in particular.

Why not live as though you realize that this is true—as though you realize that there is no separation, no distinction, between you and Reality?

If you do, there will no longer be any mystery to existence. Mystery only comes about when we wall ourselves off, divide the world into this and that, distinguish ourselves from everything else.

Reality is not a thought. Reality is not what you think. Reality is not what you *can* think. Reality is what is immediately experienced.

Reality is what it is. Truth is what it is. The real question is, what are you?

8

REBIRTH,
NOT REINCARNATION

O NE COMMON UNDERSTANDING of Buddhism is that it involves reincarnation. But if we go back to the original insights of the Buddha, we don't find this teaching. What the Buddha taught was rebirth, not reincarnation. Though they are often confused, they are not the same at all.

Our usual understanding—that we're born, persist for a time, and then die—creates a big problem for us human beings. We become frightened of our own mortality. The notion of our own death fills us with anxiety. We want to know, "What happens to me after I die? Where do I go? Or do I simply vanish?"

In response, human beings have constructed all sorts of beliefs and opinions about where we've come from and where we're going. We've created various images of heaven and hell. We have notions of nothingness and oblivion. And we sometimes come up with thoughts of reincarnation: "I'll come back as someone else." Sometimes these notions are coupled with the idea that if we're good, we can come back in more fortunate circumstances.

An ancient Hindu idea was that if you're really good, you can come back as a god. Many people—including many Buddhists—believe that if you're pretty good, but not top-notch, you can come back as a human. If not, you might come back as an animal or a plant. And if you've really blown it, you might come back as a mineral of some kind.

What all of these concepts have in common is that they suppose some enduring entity—incarnate, here and now—that persists and, after it dies, disintegrates, only to reemerge as something else again.

But there's a problem here. If it becomes something else, then in what way is it the same? How is it still, in some manner, what it used to be? And if it's not, then how is this reincarnation? Indeed, what does the term *it* even refer to?

We have no idea. How can anything be both what it is *and* something else?

Yet many of us persist in believing that there's this aspect of who we are—this soul, this self—that persists and is somehow recaptured or reembodied in future incarnations.

Here is what many people miss (or ignore) about the Buddhadharma: the Buddha himself pointed out that this view is inaccurate and extreme. It's called the eternalistic view—the view that there's an enduring self, a soul, that survives the body and persists in some fashion, perhaps through reincarnation. But the awakened *see* directly that permanence is never found, that the eternalistic view simply doesn't hold up.

This is not a matter of belief. The awakened don't hold any beliefs on this subject at all.

We need to be aware of our wishful thinking, of our leanings of mind, and of how we grasp at explanations and answers—especially those ready-made to accommodate our egoistic desires. We need to *see* how we hold to things—especially to this delicious and compelling idea of "me"—and how we're overcome with the intense desire to please, preserve, and protect this dear little self.

The Buddha said that to *see* with *right wisdom* is to *see* that nothing holds still but exhibits only thoroughgoing flux, flow, and change. When we *see* this clearly, we no longer take seriously any notion of persistence. In other words, when we look honestly at actual experience, without adding or assuming anything extra, the notion of an abiding self does not occur.

As the great thirteenth-century Japanese Zen teacher Dogen Zenji said, "Just as firewood does not revert to firewood once it burns to ash, so a person does not return to life after death." Were we somehow to come back, we could do so neither as ourselves (for we'd be someone else) nor as another (for then we'd not be ourselves).

The fact is, *within this one life span,* as we live from moment to moment, we are never a particular, unchanging person. You are not the same person you were ten or twenty years ago. In fact, you're not the person you were ten or twenty minutes ago.

Look at the hand holding this book. Even in this short span of time, "it's" not the same hand that picked it up. All the blood has been exchanged. Materials have been released and absorbed through the skin. The configurations of bone, muscle, and sinew have all changed; skin has sloughed off; nails have grown. Everything—about our bodies, our minds, and the world—has changed and will continue to do so.

Our problem stems from our deeply held assumption that the words *you*, *me*, *I*, and *it* refer to some real aspect of actual experience. But the fact is that we don't experience a singular, unchanging self. With some careful examination, we can *see* this. We can *see* that the self is a mentally constructed notion—and a contradictory one at that.

The Buddha spoke of rebirth (the full term is "rebirth consciousness"), not reincarnation. With each new moment, the universe is reborn, so to speak. Rebirth consciousness is the awareness that *this moment* is not *this* (new) *moment*. The person *here now* is not the same as this person *here* (in this newly formed moment) *now*. Nothing persists. Nothing repeats. Nothing returns. Each moment is fresh, new, unique—impermanent.

Rebirth consciousness is the conceptual glue that appears to link all these distinct moments together. Thus, instead of seeing separate frames of a movie in rapid succession, we see what appears to be an ongoing and seamless flow of moments. In other words, *this moment* looks very much like *this* (next) *moment*, which looks very much like *this* (next) *moment*. But no two moments are ever exactly the same. Instead, each moment presents a newborn universe.

Nagarjuna, the great second-century Indian Buddhist philosopher, pointed out that there's nothing persisting from moment to moment. In fact, there's nothing that endures, even the least bit, to *be* impermanent. He calls this Emptiness. This is the true meaning of impermanence.

This observation, which is based solely on immediate, direct experience, is simply incompatible with any notion of reincarnation, since reincarnation assumes the persistence of some kind of self or embodied entity. *There is no way to hold a view of reincarnation without holding a view of permanence.* Thus any view of reincarnation is antithetical to what the Buddha taught.

This moment has been born again and again, innumerable times while you've read this chapter. Learning to *see this*, and not the recycling of souls, is the liberation the Buddha pointed to.

9

THE DEEP SECRET
IN PLAIN VIEW

THERE IS A SAYING in Zen that birth and death are impermanent and swift. It's considered a secret teaching, even though its expression is found everywhere. Indeed, it's right out in the open, right in front of us all the time. We can *see* it wherever we cast our gaze. All we need to do is just *look* and we'll *see* that there's no permanence. Birth and death are found in each moment. Nothing persists at all.

Often what we look for most earnestly is right in front of us, in full view. For example, when I was a child, my mother would hide Easter eggs. My brother and I would look behind curtains, under chairs, and inside lamps, but invariably it was the eggs she'd leave in the most conspicuous places, right out in the open, that we'd find last.

It's the same for us right *now*. Although we might think we're seeking Truth, we're not looking carefully at what's actually taking place. We're caught by our thinking, our desires, our wants, our fears, our sense of self. All of these serve to remove us from the actual immediate, direct experience of *this moment*. It's all out in the open, but we're not really *looking*. Instead, we're focused on what we think—and on what we expect to find.

Because we're so caught up in our intellectualizing, our emotions, and our mental constructions, the objects of our concern seem compellingly real for us—and gripping. Furthermore, virtually everyone around us is caught in the same way. Thus we create shared delusions.

We also have our own individual delusions, of course. That we put things together differently, forming our own points of view, shows the subtlety with which our personal story lines keep us separate and removed from the events we blithely assume they capture. Because we hold to these tightly, even though Reality unfolds before us, we're not paying attention. We settle into our ideas and beliefs about what's happening and miss what's actually going on. Thus we become captive spectators of the delicious and frightening things and thoughts that seem to come and go before us.

The fact is, though, that nothing's holding still, even for a moment. Impermanence is so thorough that we can't even say there's something that's actually changing. Nothing forms or holds still long enough *to* change. It's not simply that the world exhibits impermanence or that impermanence is an attribute of it. It's that *this moment—now—*in which everything appears is impermanence itself.

When we look carefully at actual experience, we don't find a world in constant flux and change. Rather, we find only flux and change, which themselves are what we call the world. (Of course, "flux" and "change" are not things or concepts or even processes. They are simply *thus*.)

The Buddha pointed out that any idea of existence or persistence is faulty. But he also pointed out that any notion of nonexistence is also flawed.

Many people think that the Buddhadharma teaches that all is impermanent, that everything in the universe is in constant change, being born and dying endlessly. But this is not exactly what the Buddha taught (nor is it borne out by actual experience). Rather, he *saw* that there isn't *anything* that comes or goes, that is born or dies.

If we reach into this world where things appear to come and go and try to find something to put our mind at ease, to free us from our pain, suffering, and confusion, we'll not find it.

Instead, we will find it only in *this moment*—in the complete freedom and fluidity of impermanence itself.

10

THE WARP AND
WOOF OF REALITY

A LONG THE COAST of Brazil, the ancient mangroves are being destroyed for hotels and other real estate development. Sixty percent of the mangroves are now gone, and the rest are disappearing at a rapid rate.

The nutrients washing down the rivers used to filter into the mangroves, providing a rich habitat that supported an abundance of life. With the mangroves disappearing, such wealth is now being largely flushed out to sea; much of what remains is dying.

Offshore, the coral reefs are also dying because all the silt that was once caught by the mangroves is now being carried out to sea, where it eventually settles, covering the reefs. As a result, the coral can't get enough sunlight. And with the reefs dying, much of the aquatic life that depends on the reefs is dying as well.

At the present rate of destruction, all the mangroves worldwide will be gone in ten years. How many living things today are alive simply because this planet has had mangroves for millions of years? And how many of these species do we rely on to sustain us now? We have no idea.

In Reality, everything is interconnected. We can't afford to separate out any of it. The fabric of what is Real has too tight a weave. Nothing can be removed or thrown away. It's all *here,* and it remains *here.* And it all functions in harmony, without requiring any managerial help from us.

This points to one of the most subtle and profound insights of the Buddha. It has to do with our will, our intent.

Not only do we not need to manage things in nature, the fact is that we can't. And if we try to, we typically make a mess of it because we've operated out of our dualistic thought. Though we don't intend to, and don't realize what we've done, in trying to manage nature we defy how the natural world operates.

Nature isn't dualistic. It isn't merely a collection of separate parts. It doesn't throw anything away. It recycles everything. And it doesn't operate out of a desire to improve things. While *we* fixate on the parts, nature acts out of the Whole.

We need to start recognizing that the world itself is not dualistic. We need to appreciate that our dualistic thinking doesn't match Reality and that we pay a heavy and painful price for this discrepancy. Only then can we learn to live on this Earth without making a mess of it.

It's not that we have to keep our hands off everything. We can't do that, anyway; after all, we're part and parcel of it. But we can learn to act in accord with Reality.

11

NEITHER SACRED
NOR PROFANE

O NE OF THE CLASSIC Zen teachings is "no dualism."
But what does this mean, exactly?

Dualism is our separating the world into this and that, self
and other, good and bad, right and wrong. To the extent that
we conceptualize, dualism is right here. And while dualism has
a legitimate place in our lives—it helps us communicate with
one another and function in a multifaceted world—it can never
be an accurate representation of Reality, let alone Reality itself.

In fact, dualistic thinking gets us into all kinds of troubling
and painful situations. It leads us into worry, fear, anxiety, and
confusion. But it doesn't have to be this way. For, while we
habitually think in dualistic terms, we never actually live in
dualism.

It's not that dualism is bad or wrong. It's just that we easily
get stuck in it, believing that the way we've framed everything
in our thoughts is how things actually are. We think that the

way we account for things in our minds—the way we separate things out from one another—somehow gives us a handle on Reality. As a result, we regularly operate in ways that are completely out of touch with how things actually are.

For example, we see some things as sacred or holy and other things as worldly or profane. We separate the transcendent from the mundane, belief from ignorance, insight from delusion. Yet in doing so, we fall right back into the same habit of dualistic thinking. With this assumption we ripen ourselves for contention with others, with the world, and even with ourselves.

This is why Bodhidharma, the Brahmin who brought Zen to China in the fifth century C.E., said that holding dualistic views of ordinary and enlightened does not accord with the teaching of the Awakened.

According to Bodhidharma (and to Zen), if we make enlightenment—or enlightened people—into something special and set them apart from others and from ourselves, we abuse them. In the process, we also abuse ourselves. Thus enlightenment becomes remote, otherworldly, mysterious, and (seemingly) virtually impossible to realize.

Zen is about freeing ourselves from such deluded thinking.

This isn't to say that distinctions cannot be made between ordinary and enlightened. But we have to realize that such distinctions take place only within our minds. No such distinctions actually occur in Reality.

There's never any particular person who is enlightened. Enlightenment doesn't work that way. By the same token, there's never any particular person who is deluded, either. We only think there is. Indeed, the very notion of a "particular person" is dualistic—provisionally useful for getting through the day, certainly, but nevertheless not reflective of Reality.

As we become familiar with Buddhist teachings, we often get the idea that enlightenment is the ultimate prize. Then we naturally start to think, "That's what I want. That's what I'm after. This is why I'm taking up this practice of meditation and studying these teachings—so that I can attain enlightenment."

Such thinking is just more dualism, more delusion. Zen teachers, both ancient and modern, tell us repeatedly, in many different ways, that if this is our thinking, it's out of tune with Reality.

Typically we hear this, we take it in intellectually, and we even nod in agreement—but we don't take it to heart. We think about dualism and project it "out there," as though it were somebody else's problem. We say, "Oh, yes, dualism. It's not good." Thus we apply an extra layer of dualism to the subject of dualism itself. And all the while, we don't look at where we stand.

We need to digest this teaching and take it to heart. We need to realize in each moment what this teaching is pointing to— and what we're doing with it instead.

We can't actually say what Truth or Reality is. Whatever we *do* say is dualistic by virtue of the fact that it's been verbalized, put into conceptual form.

Zen teaching goes beyond any merely intellectual under-standing. We need to come back to this repeatedly and soak in it so we can truly digest it and practice it.

We can learn to come back to *this moment*. We can start to recognize our dualistic thinking as it takes place within our mind. We can learn to *see* our grasping and judging. We can *see* how we reach for what we deem sacred and how we spurn what we imagine to be profane.

When we *see* how we do this, we can also learn to *see* how not to get caught up in it.

Our thinking and conceptualizing, far from giving us a handle on Truth, obstruct our natural ability to *see* Reality di-rectly. Our thinking—no matter how or what we think—is out of step with how things actually are. Once you *see* this for yourself, you will stop endlessly frustrating yourself by trying to figure out what's going on. It will be obvious that whatever conceptual answer you come up with will be dualistic, while Reality is not. It will also be obvious that what is needed is not an answer or explanation but only direct *seeing*.

Truth isn't an idea or a belief. It isn't graspable. It isn't even conceivable. Still, it can be directly *seen*.

Little by little, we can acquire a taste of just what's True and Real—understanding that it's neither sacred nor profane. We can learn to *see* it directly without requiring an explanation for it.

The fact is, Truth is something we already *know;* we only need to come back to it and settle down. We only need to be reminded of it.

12

CANYONS IN A CUP

ZEN PRACTICE is about being awake, being aware. But if the point is to be awake, what do we do about it? How do we wake up? And what does it mean to be awake? Aren't we awake now?

Huang Po, a Chinese Zen master of the seventh century C.E., said,

> If you students of the Way do not awake to this Mind, you will overlay Mind with conceptual thought. You will seek Buddha outside yourselves, and you will remain attached to forms, pious practices and so on—all of which are harmful and not at all the way to supreme Knowledge.

This is precisely what we do. We overlay our direct experience of Reality with our *ideas* of what is real. And because our ability to do this is so subtle and so highly developed, we don't even know we're doing it. Thus we become chronically confused.

Take any object—a mountain, the sky, or an everyday object like a teacup. Our usual way is to think, "It's just a cup." Often we know the object so well, and we size it up so quickly, that we ignore it almost entirely. We make ourselves a pot of tea and blindly fill the cup with no thought and barely any awareness of what we're actually doing. We do this because we "know"—we believe—it's just a cup and nothing more.

But if we really pay attention to what's actually experienced, it's not just a cup. If we look, we can see the whole universe right here, as this cup. Inside this cup, as the Sufi poet Kabir would say, "are canyons and pine mountains."

The cup doesn't appear by itself. Someone took clay and fashioned it. And someone made that potter's wheel. And there's the tree that fueled the fire for the kiln. And the sun and the rain and the soil that grew the tree.

When we see that all this has gone into the picture, we can then actually experience a cup. We can *see* the cup for what it is—which is to say that it really isn't anything in particular.

Try to nail down what anything is. You can't. It's like trying to answer the question, "Is that you in your baby picture?" What can you say? You may say, "Yes, that's me." But obviously it is not. You're not a baby. But can you say, "No"? Who is it in the picture, then?

And if you say, "That *was* me," how could you still be you if you're six times bigger and far more articulate? Indeed, what does "you" refer to? And if you say, "It's both me and not me," what can this mean? Have you ever seen anything that both is and isn't what it is? And if it's neither you nor not you, what are we even talking about? If we really look carefully, such simple, everyday questions as these can set our minds spinning.

There's nothing absolute about our objects, ever, even though we usually think there is. We quietly assume a cup is a cup is a cup. But where can we draw the line between the cup and everything else? If you pay very close attention, you'll see that you can't.

Anything you can package in your mind, anything you can frame and divide from other things, is a concept. And confusing our concepts with Reality is what gets us into so much trouble.

Once again the question becomes, how do we wake up?

First of all, you have to want to wake up. But wanting to wake up is not like wanting a new car or a new job or respect or love. If you really want to wake up, these other things are irrelevant. To want in this way is not ordinary wanting. If you want to wake up to how the world really is, you must be totally open to *this*—the Reality of *this moment*—even while knowing full well that you can't conceive of how it really is. Waking up can only come about through *seeing*, not through coercion or the application of will. It requires a willingness to let go of all your cherished opinions.

To seek enlightenment as though we expect some kind of payback is only to frustrate ourselves. If you really want to wake up, then just wake up.

Start paying attention to your objects. Notice what you're thinking, believing, conceiving—what you're constructing in your mind. And start to notice how baffling and contradictory and pervasive the constructions of your mind really are.

Once we really understand what's going on, we're less likely to hang on to our cherished opinions because we can now *see* that everything we pick up is like water trickling out between our fingers. We know we're not going to get too far with our mental constructions before they all fall apart and no longer work.

The universe is not mysterious. Reality is clearly displayed at all times. Nothing is hidden. But for our thoughts we would *see* it.

The True Path is meeting your eyes even now. Just attend to what is actually going on—but keep it simple and keep it clear. Just open your wisdom eye and *see*.

13

JUST SEEING

I HAVE NEVER written a word before *now*.

This is literally true. If, however, I announced this to most people, they would doubt my sanity. Or else they would hear it as one of those ostensibly zany, bewildering Zen statements.

In fact, however, such expressions aren't (and aren't meant to be) zany or bewildering at all.

To help people wake up, Zen teachers often use words and concepts to point to Reality, which, though it can be *seen* directly, is impossible to describe or conceptalize. As a result, they sometimes say seemingly contradictory things—silly things, ridiculous things.

These kinds of statements are easy to imitate. But they're also easy to misunderstand.

This is why Zen teachers often test each other's insight. Otherwise, it would seem that all you have to do to teach Zen is learn to rattle off a lot of outlandish, irrational statements.

But true Zen teachers don't simply throw out idiotic statements. They're dead serious.

So in Zen we have a history of teachers checking their students' understanding—and checking out each others'. A typical encounter might run something like this:

It's late evening. The teacher says to a student, "Show me your Zen." (In other words, "Show me your understanding.")

The student leans near the teacher and turns on his lamp.

The teacher barks back disapprovingly, "Is that all you understand?"

The student makes the perfect move by leaning over once again and turning off the lamp.

The teacher smiles or nods approvingly, knowing the student has demonstrated genuine insight.

This is a fairly typical exchange. Easy to imitate. But it's not that easy to trick a Zen master. Instead of nodding approval, the teacher might start prodding and probing. For instance, when you lean over to turn off the lamp, the teacher might ask, "Is the light on or off?" What will you say? (If you're reaching for the right response, you're already in trouble.)

Zen is about *just seeing*. If we know how to *just see* without adding any thought or calculation to what's *seen*, we'll not have any problem. When a Zen teacher tests someone, they're checking out their ability to *just see* (although *ability* is a misleading term, since all of us are already fully capable of *seeing* already).

Just seeing can be demonstrated in numberless ways. None of them, however, involves knowing, finding, or looking for the right answer. In fact, if you're thinking in terms of "the right answer," you're already off the mark. (Actually, if you're thinking at all, you're off the mark because you're conceptualizing, not *seeing*.)

What does it mean to *just see?*

Here's an experiment that might give you a backward sense of *just seeing* by showing how we usually approach the world with prepackaged notions, assumptions, expectations, concepts, and inclinations. The analogy isn't perfect, since it remains conceptual; nevertheless, you may get a taste of it.

First, relax and get comfortable. Breathe deeply for a moment or two, and let your mind calm.

Now, look at the ink blotches on the next page. They depict something quite familiar to you. Just look at them for a while.

Recognize it? No? Look again.

If, after a minute or two, you haven't seen what the picture depicts, try rotating it ninety degrees to the right. Look some more. Don't try to figure anything out; there's nothing to be figured out here. Either you will see what you're looking at or you won't. When you do see, you won't have any doubts.

If, after another moment or two, you're still stumped, try making the shape of the central white portion your main object of interest rather than the black blotches. Keep looking.

Eventually you may realize that what you're looking at is a crude reverse silhouette of much of western Europe. In the lower left (assuming you've already rotated the picture ninety degrees) is a portion of Spain; in the lower right is most of Italy (minus the telltale "boot"); the southernmost part of England is in the upper left, across the (black) English Channel from France.

In retrospect, all of these details may seem obvious. Certainly they were right there in front of you, unobscured, ready to be seen all along. If you've got a reasonable amount of geographic knowledge, why didn't you immediately see what the picture was?

You didn't because all of us observe things in habitual ways. In this instance, we're used to taking small dark shapes as our focus of interest; thus, naturally, our calculating eyes go to them first as we try to make sense of them.

Also, even in the case of something familiar, such as an outline of western Europe, we're used to a particular orientation. Without this, we lose many of the clues we rely on to construct the world in our minds.

We all have conceptual habits such as these that help us make sense of the world. But these habits also limit us; they can throw us off, as they did with the picture of western Europe or as they do with optical illusions. This habit of framing and encapsulating and viewing things in certain ways is conceptualizing. Thus, it is not *just seeing* but is, rather, in sharp contrast to it.

When you first approached the map, you may have had a chance to *just see*—that is, perceive directly, before concepts arose and your habit of trying to sort things out took over. Once we lay meaning and significance on what's *seen*, however, we no longer *just see*. At this point we take our observation and read into it what is not there, weaving in and out of our perceptual experience and our conceptual overlay. We do this so automatically and with such ease that we rarely even notice that we do it.

A buddha, an awakened person, is someone who *just sees*—that is, someone who does not confuse conception with perception.

Pure perception is an objectless Awareness. It's prior to all our mental formations, our packaging of experience into things, thoughts, and feelings—and into "I" and "that."

What most distinguishes a buddha from an ordinary person has to do with this matter of *just seeing*. There is no difference between the perception of a buddha and the rest of us. The difference lies in how a buddha deals with concepts that naturally arise. A buddha doesn't confuse thinking with *seeing*, and neither does a buddha let a thought or concept override perception.

When we're caught up in what we think, we can't be clear about what we *see*, though this is rarely obvious to us. Instead of *just seeing*, most of us most of the time search for a better idea, a more useful concept, a clearer explanation that will at last crack open the world for us.

But the world doesn't need cracking open. It's open already. Neither does it need (nor can it possibly have) any explanation, as if it were a puzzle or a formula or an equation.

Reality is actually very familiar to all of us. It's only because we're so easily and continuously caught up in our thoughts and conceptual habits that we miss it.

Bearing all this in mind, let's return to that question about the light. Is it on or off? In our phenomenal world—our mentally constructed model of Reality—it would seem that it's got to be one or the other. Not only that, but this would seem indisputable. Like our habit of looking for meaning in the small dark shapes on the page, this is how we see things. Everything is neatly packaged in distinct terms. And so, a light with an up-down toggle switch must be either on or off.

But this is a highly conceptual way of seeing. Here's "on," which is completely distinct and separate from "off." If we would *just see*, however, without laying on a lot of assumptions of substance, materiality, otherness, and a host of other notions—most of which are unexamined and unacknowledged—we'd understand that our conceptual view is not the Whole picture.

We overlook that we cannot have "off" without "on." We cannot have "this" without "that." In fact, no object can form in the mind without its very identity being wrapped up in all that it is not.

With perception, everything appears as intimate and close. Nothing gets left out. There's nothing "coming in" from "outside," as it were. It's only through our conceptualizing that we have the impression we're taking things in from "out there." Thus, with bare attention, it becomes obvious that for anything to appear within our conceptual experience at all, everything that is not the momentary object of our interest is necessarily taking part. If concave shows up, convex is there as well, and the Universe is filled.

All things are like this. Indeed, it's impossible for any conceived object not to be like this. Nothing stands on its own. Nothing has its own being. Each thing is inseparable from, and inter-identical with, all that it's not.

Thus perception is an objectless Awareness since, when we *just see*, what is truly *seen* involves not objects but the Whole. Nothing actually forms as an object; nothing stands apart. No matter where we *look*, there's *just this*.

Here's another example of a foolish-sounding Zen question that is actually an expression of *just seeing:* What is the sound of one hand clapping?

When we conceive of a hand, it's just a single, isolated hand, and we're puzzled at the question. To clap, we need two hands. But this is approaching the question in our ordinary way—that is, conceptually.

With naked perception, however, we *see* that a hand is not a separate and distinct hand. Everything is included with it. One hand clapping is the sound of two hands clapping is the sound of ten hands clapping. It's the sound before and after two hands clap. It's also the sound before and after one hand claps.

Conceptually, we think that sound is sound and silence is silence. The two seem neatly separated and distinct—in fact, opposite of each other. But this is only how we think, how we conceptualize. This is not how Reality is perceived, before we put everything into neat, nicely labeled (but deceptive) little packages.

We think there only has to be sound for there to be sound. We overlook that there must also be silence for there to be sound. And because of sound, there is silence. Were there no sound, how could there be silence?

Before you strike a bell, sound is already *here*. After you strike the bell, the sound is *here*. When the sound fades and dies away, the sound is still *here*. The sound is not just the sound but the silence, too. And the silence is the sound. This is what is actually perceived *before* we parse everything out into this and that, into "myself" and "what I hear."

The sound of the bell is inseparable from everything that came before and that will come after as well as from everything that appears *now*. This includes your eardrum, which vibrates in response to it. It includes the air, which pulses with varying waves of pressure in response to it. It includes the stick that strikes the bell. It includes the metallurgists, past and present, and those who learned to extract metal from ore and those who fashioned the bell. And it includes that ancient furnace, that supernova obliterated long ago in which this metal formed. Remove any of these—indeed, remove anything at all—and there can be no sound of the bell. The sound of the bell is thus not "the sound of the bell." It is the entire Universe.

As I said at the beginning of this chapter, I have never written a word before *now*. As we ordinarily see things, this is ridiculous. Nevertheless, it's True.

According to our conceptualizing minds, things persist and endure over time. Thus, according to how we conceive things, the "me" of fifty years ago or five years ago or five days ago or five minutes ago are all the same as the "me" *right now*. But that's ridiculous. Fifty years ago, what I'm calling "me" was a child. In what way is that the "me" of five minutes ago? And where are we supposed to find the "me" of five minutes—or fifty years—ago? Try as we might, we'll find no such entity anywhere—not *now*, not *here*.

How can I say that *I've* written anything before *now* when *this* "I" appears only *now*, never in the past?

We think we go home to the same room, house, or apartment every night. But this is not the full picture; it's merely how we've conceptualized our experience. Every night—

indeed, every moment—is a different experience: a different you, a different house, a different pet or roommate or spouse or child. Each meal is a meal never eaten before, in a world that's not the same as last night or even the moment before.

To *just see* is to release the tight grip we unwittingly place on everything we think.

You have never read a word before *now*. *Just see* that this is so, and taste freedom.

14

THE REVELATION
OF THE WORLD

I WAS IN THE Boundary Waters Canoe Area Wilderness, sitting alone in my canoe on calm, glassy water. There was no wind, and all was restful and still. A slight undulation in the water threw the low, soft morning light into the rocks and trees on the shore. It was exquisitely beautiful and quiet. A bird called from the wood; a loon swam by very close, probably a little curious about what I was doing. An eagle dove for a fish. Missed.

Ju-ching, Dogen's teacher in China, told Dogen before he returned to Japan that he should stay away from the hurly-burly of human affairs. Ju-ching urged him to go out of the city into nature, into wildness. That's ultimately what Dogen did. He founded Eiheiji monastery in a remote area of Japan. It's fairly remote even today.

There is tranquillity in the countryside. It's peaceful. It's quiet. It isn't the clamorous and distracting life of the city.

And so, when we go there, we calm down and center ourselves more easily.

This seems pretty obvious. And we might think that it's the sole reason for going there to practice meditation. But if this is all we've got in mind, we're missing a far more subtle point.

For one thing, the countryside isn't always tranquil. Even though it was very peaceful on my canoe trip, the fact is that storms can come up. I've been in that same wilderness when the weather's been frightening. I've seen wind, rain, and hail topple large trees. In fact, a storm passed through the area the very next summer that toppled virtually all the large pines I had seen. Where those stately pines had stood is now a tangle of brush so thick that even the rocks are no longer visible. Here and there massive trunks still rise, but they've all been snapped off about ten or fifteen feet above the ground. And along a portage nearby, large cedars, some as old as six hundred years, have fallen from the wind.

The peace and tranquillity we want to find don't come to us just because we go to the countryside. The peacefulness we cultivate in Zen practice is not something to be imported from outside ourselves.

Placing ourselves in a quiet environment may be helpful, at least at the beginning of our Zen practice. In these early stages it's easy to become distracted by sounds and events around us. So if we go to a place that offers quietude, perhaps we find it easier to settle down.

But if we have to rely on the outside world being quiet for us to find peace and tranquillity of mind, we're going to be frequently frustrated and our practice isn't going to be very solid or grounded. For the fact is that at any moment, whether we're in the city or the country, disturbances can appear, sometimes without warning.

Hakuin, an eighteenth-century Japanese Zen teacher, displayed this peace, tranquillity, and stability of mind regardless of his circumstances. Once, a young woman in his village accused him—falsely—of being the father of her baby, and her parents went to Hakuin to confront him. He didn't dispute their story or argue with them. All he said was, "Is that so?" He remained peaceful and stable, even as his reputation as a monk and teacher was destroyed.

When the baby was born, the grandparents brought him to Hakuin. They told him, "It's yours. You take care of it." Without complaint, he took the baby and began tending to all his needs.

In time, however, the truth came out. The young mother confessed that the father was actually the young man down at the fish market. So once again, her parents went to see Hakuin to take the baby back.

After taking care of this baby for a year, Hakuin freely gave him up. "Is that so?" was all Hakuin said as he turned the baby over to his grandparents.

If we want to cultivate Hakuin's flexibility and stability of mind, we need to stop looking for these qualities in the outside world—or, rather, in what we think of as the outside world.

. . .

One of my teacher's main themes throughout his career was wholehearted practice. I heard it from him over and over. It took time for me to realize he was talking about *this present moment*—not just zazen (sitting meditation), but the practice that is our whole life. In other words, we need to live our lives wholeheartedly, with our eyes open. Or, as Thoreau said, we must live life deliberately.

Katagiri Roshi used to say that Zen was either zero or one hundred percent. In other words, whatever you do, do it wholeheartedly or not at all. Don't enter into any activity with a halfhearted mind. Whatever you do must be fully expressed within yourself and your life or not at all.

In committing to this practice, this attitude, this intention, you'll find Hakuin's tranquillity and stability of mind. Then, as the storms of life come and go, like Hakuin, you'll know the way to ride them through. And instead of relying on something "out there" to give you calmness and stability, you'll be relying on the calmness and stability you've cultivated within yourself. You'll have taken this teaching and this practice to heart, and you'll have learned to express them, over and over, in each moment.

Unexpected, surprising, and even traumatic events may occur at any time. When they do, you won't run from them. And you'll notice that true calmness and stability don't depend on the world outside.

So Ju-ching gave his recommendation to Dogen not because he thought Dogen would find calmness and stability of mind "out there." We can look deeper—to an awareness characterized by Thoreau's famous quote: "In wildness is the preservation of the world."

In the city, for better or worse, everything is planned. Everything is put there for some purpose—for good or ill, convenience or decoration.

Nature, on the other hand, is unintentional. Nature doesn't try to do anything, produce anything, or accomplish anything.

Nevertheless, nature does produce a great deal. But nature produces things in a radically different way than human beings generally do. Most human actions come out of our intentions, our desires, our attempts to bring about certain situations, and our yearning to prevent other situations from occurring. In contrast, what nature produces is without purpose, intention, or will. This is because there is nothing outside of nature for it to act on or for or against.

So I would modify Thoreau's words and say that in wildness is not only the preservation of the world, but the revelation of the world.

Often we imagine that there's some particular thing or entity—God, say—that made the world and that now runs it. With such a notion in place, we soon start talking about this entity as if it had attributes like us—as if it had wants and desires. We talk of the "will of God." Soon we're developing ideas of how people should comply with God's will.

But if we look carefully at this, we'll discover that this is just our putting our ideas of God—that is, our will—onto unwilled nature, onto Reality. If we think of God—or whatever overarching principle we might have in mind—as being "out there," we should realize that all we are doing is projecting our own attitude, our own view, our own small mind, on the world and on others.

The intention and will that we find surging within us, which all too often govern our minds and justify our motivations for doing this or not doing that, come about because we're locked up in our petty egos, because we forsake the Reality of the Whole. We see ourselves separate and removed from the Whole—and from everything else "out there." Thus we feel compelled to do something about our situation, which only furthers our discontent.

We feel we have to protect this well-loved thing we call "me" or "I." And we also want to please this I-creature. And so we find ourselves filled with longing and loathing.

This is delusion. It's what most often characterizes our minds. We don't recognize that our way out of such sorrow is simply to *see*—not to fix something "out there."

If we would wake up and *see*, we'd call this *seeing* enlightened Mind. But we shouldn't think we can retain our separate identity and have this kind of Mind.

In fact, the enlightened Mind has us. Even now, it has us all. It already holds everything that we see, hear, feel, and think. It is the Mind of the Whole, of Reality itself.

There is nothing outside this Mind. Hence, unlike our personal minds, which are so filled with longing and loathing, it doesn't lean toward or away from anything. It doesn't try to bring about anything in particular. Unlike our egoistically created notions of God, the Mind of the Whole—that is, Reality—is without will.

As things rise up out of this world of difference and separation—things that can seem threatening and displeasing to the ordinary human mind—just *see,* as Hakuin did, that there is nothing you need to reach for and nothing you need to recoil from.

The heart of Ju-ching's advice to Dogen was to remove himself from the intentional world we completely surround ourselves with. Otherwise, we're caught up in our petty thoughts —our likes, our dislikes, our preoccupations, our prejudices— busily brooding over all the things that displease us or that we feel we must have.

To the extent that we can remove ourselves from this world of longing and loathing that we create for ourselves, we make it easier to see how we get caught up in our own spinning minds. We can then begin to realize that Zen practice has to do with simplifying our lives, with not being taken in by this or tossed about by that. We can start to *see* that it's not in the world "out there" that we get caught, but in our own minds— within our own attitudes and assumptions and emotions.

We might think it is easier to see the world as illusion when we're in an artificial environment. Not so. When we're in the artificial, human-made environment of the city, we generally forget about the world altogether. We forget about the Reality of this moment. We get caught up with things and thoughts and issues. We adopt a businesslike mind—a purposeful mind, a calculating mind, a mind busily defending or pleasing an illusory self.

But when we remove ourselves from the dizzy life of getting and spending and place ourselves in a natural, unintentional environment—when we just sit quietly in a canoe on calm water, watching low light undulating in the trees and over the rocks—it's much easier to see that it's all illusion.

By *illusion*, I don't mean that water and trees and rocks and canoes aren't real, exactly. They just aren't "real" in the way we think they are—as discrete, persisting entities separated out from the Whole and from each other and from us.

We might think, "But the natural environment is what's real! It's our artificial environment that's illusory. After all, we created it. We thought it up." But that's not what makes it illusion. It was already illusion even before we tried to control it. And once we get busy manipulating things, it becomes harder for us to *see* that the True nature of the world is illusion because we're so easily caught up in our creations.

Of course, whether we try to take hold of it and control it or *just see* it, it's all the same Reality. It's all being handled by the Whole—by nature.

Illusion isn't bad or wrong or evil. Our problem is not that we must somehow extricate ourselves from illusion or from the world. That's not what Zen practice is about. It's about finally realizing what it is about the world that is illusory. This is much easier to do when you're in a setting, or a state of mind, that isn't constantly pulling you away and engaging you in some purpose.

In Zen practice, our focus is not on going "out there" to get something or to fix our circumstances or to straighten things out. Instead, our focus is on our own mind. Notice how this thing or that or the next constantly jerks you around in a myriad of subtle ways. Notice what *this* moment is and how it comes about. Notice how your inattention keeps you from actually *seeing* what's going on.

Notice that awakening, your natural home, is clear and obvious.

15

LIBERATION, NOT RESIGNATION

T HE BUDDHA SAID that he taught only two things: *duk-kha*—which can be translated as change, sorrow, loss, suffering, vexation, or confusion—and release from *dukkha*.

As long as we hold tightly to our dear self, *dukkha* is ever with us. In fact, if we look carefully, we can *see* that even pleasure involves *dukkha* because, as things change, we suffer the loss (and the fear of loss) of pleasure.

Basically, then, *dukkha* is human life. It's also bondage.

The Buddha pointed out this bondage and a way to be free from it. This freedom occurs in recognizing how, through ignorance, we bind ourselves in thought.

By showing us in detail how we get entangled and ensnared in myriad things, situations, and relationships, the Buddha's teachings can help us avoid a great deal of suffering, including the unsettling sense that at bottom we haven't a clue about what's going on.

But the Buddha didn't stop there. He went on to show how we can be free even of this—free even of liberation and enlightenment.

We're very confused about freedom. We spout all kinds of ideas about it, but those notions are all actually forms of bondage, precisely *because* they're just ideas that we've substituted for Reality. Thus we have a difficult time truly tasting freedom because the more we think about it, chase after it, and try to reach it or acquire it, the more we only thwart our efforts by throwing ourselves back into bondage. In trying to obtain freedom, we perpetuate our confusion and suffering.

Some people think the Buddha said that we should just give in and accept the difficulties of life. They think he basically told people, "Listen, just don't let it bother you. The human situation is always vexing and difficult; all you can do is get by as best you can."

In fact, however, the Buddha said nothing of the sort. Indeed, he acknowledged that people would often misunderstand and misinterpret him. He even said, "What I call liberation, the world calls resignation."

Then there are people, even some Buddhists, who think that the best Buddhism can offer is to bring us to a place of internal peace. For them, the goal is to be able to say, "I have finally found peace."

But when the Buddha spoke of liberation, he was not talking about such a dismal and limited experience.

The Buddha taught genuine liberation, authentic freedom of mind; he showed us how to be free—not just resigned or peaceful—no matter what the circumstances.

If we don't *see*, then whatever we take up, even the Buddha's teaching itself, becomes bondage. This bondage occurs within our own mind. Thus it's within our mind—our understanding and our ability to *just see*—that we are able to realize true freedom.

In this freedom, this *seeing*, there's nothing to sacrifice. The stuff we hold to so dearly—what we fear we might be called on to give up—brings pain only because we hold on to it in the first place. But if we look closely, we'll discover that nothing is gained from holding on.

What can we actually take hold of, anyway? Nothing. Not our possessions, our thoughts, our feelings, our memories, our minds, our lives, not even those we love. Nothing abides. It will all change. Thus we don't really sacrifice anything for freedom, precisely because those things we fear giving up are things we never actually had in the first place. We only imagine we had them.

Only when we think that the stuff we grasp and cling to and chase after will satisfy us—and when we believe that we *can* take hold of stuff and that doing so will somehow answer the deep ache of our heart—only then do we tremble at the thought that it all will pass away, including our own dear self.

And it *will* all pass away, but not because you have to give it up. It will all pass away regardless of what you do. And if you don't try to hold on to any of it in the first place, you'll *see* liberation, just as the Buddha spoke of it.

Liberation comes from *seeing* deeply the True situation we're in. It never involves having something and then sacrificing it. That very notion is a bogus fear based in delusion. How could you possibly sacrifice something you never had (and only imagined you had) in the first place?

All we have to do is *see* what's really taking place in each moment. Things will then reveal themselves as the ephemera that they are and always were. Nothing is lost.

If any of this sounds a little threatening, it's only because you're still holding on to your sense of self, your sense of other.

The Truth is that we've been in this situation all along. So there's nothing to fear about pursuing this path and nothing to give up or throw away. True, something does drop away, something that may have seemed important to us while we were caught in our delusion. But upon our *seeing*, it drops away freely on its own, and it is never missed.

It's much like fearing the bogeyman. As long as we fear this nonexistent fellow, we remain bound to keeping him at bay. Perhaps we have to nail our closet door shut each night. Or we have to say incantations and prayers to keep him away. Or we must keep the lights on and stay awake lest he visit.

And we even get comfortable doing this because it's always worked. The bogeyman has never come. Consider what horrors might befall us if we were to slip up or forget. Besides, keeping him at bay is what we're used to doing. Why rock the boat? The thought of not doing something about the bogeyman fills us with fear and anxiety.

Were someone to come and silence our rituals, pull the nails from our closet door, and open it wide, we might think them crazy or at least very powerful and brave.

But, of course, they're neither, which is what we'd see for ourselves once the door was opened in the night. Suddenly we'd see that we had been in a kind of bondage, wanting and craving safety, bound up with fear and sorrow—and all of our own making.

We'd see that nothing needed to be sacrificed at all in exchange for complete and total relief. All the effort, the constant struggle to keep the bogeyman at bay—something that seemed imperative before—has now completely dropped away.

Liberation is not just about acceptance, either.

When it comes to Reality, we have no choice. We're already in the midst of Reality. It's not a matter of saying, "Okay, I accept Reality." Whether you accept it or not, Reality is Reality. We're stuck with it. Of course, we can always kick and scream, but what's the point?

What the Buddha taught is far more subtle and profound than mere acceptance. For acceptance can occur only when we imagine ourselves to be separate, cut off, isolated. Both acceptance and resignation take place only in the world of ego, where we're bound up in notions of separation.

But when we *see* what's really taking place—that the actual events of our immediate experience are not separate or removed from us—we realize that there's nothing to accept and nothing to resign ourselves to. There's also no "I" to do the accepting or resigning.

Liberation—what's going on *right here, right now*—is far beyond any notion we may have about acceptance or resignation. In fact, in liberation it becomes clear that there's no separate person to be liberated, nor is there anything to be liberated from. To *see* this is to be free.

16

THE HOST
WITHIN THE HOST

THE ESSENCE OF ZEN is *knowing* freedom.

Even though we might think we're free, most of us are bound—by our ideas, our beliefs, our concepts, our intellectualizations. As a result, we're imprisoned in a far more difficult and pernicious way than if we were behind steel bars. Yet no one imprisons us but ourselves.

Often people approach Zen in ways that only bind them all the more. We run to Zen with an urgent desire to be free and with a lot of notions about what freedom is. Then we implore the teacher to show us how to be free.

But the freedom Zen points to cannot be gained, earned, achieved, developed, or acquired. In fact, the freedom Zen points to cannot even be successfully sought. This is because freedom is already ours, right from the very start. The only reason we don't realize this is that we heap chains upon ourselves. And we do it in many and varied ways.

It's not just intellectually that we bind ourselves. We do so emotionally as well. The poet Basho beautifully expresses this kind of bondage in a haiku. Upon hearing the *hototogisu*, a cuckoolike bird known for its soft, nostalgic call, Basho wrote:

> *I am in Kyoto*
> *Yet at the voice of the Hototogisu*
> *Longing for Kyoto*

Here's Basho in the beautiful city of Kyoto. He hears the call of the hototogisu. Suddenly he feels a deep longing welling up from his heart. But he longs for Kyoto—the *idea* of Kyoto—even as he's *in* Kyoto.

We all have such feelings at times. I've known such a feeling, lying awake in my tent at night in the Boundary Waters Canoe Area Wilderness, a beloved place I've returned to year after year for the better part of my life. When I hear the haunting call of a loon, there comes a deep longing in my heart for the Boundary Waters. Yet here I am, in the Boundary Waters already.

On the other hand, this suffering of Basho's (and mine) is very beautiful. It's a form of pleasure. Yet it's still suffering, still delusion.

So how can we live lives that are free of delusion?

We can't. It's impossible. To the extent that we envision self and other, we necessarily live in a sea of delusion. We have a technical term for this in Zen. We call it "muddy water."

But delusion isn't wrong or bad. Indeed, Zen is not about trying to get rid of delusion. Delusion doesn't go away. Muddy water is muddy water. If we try to get rid of it, we only stir it up all the more.

Buddhas don't get rid of delusion; they *just see* it for what it is and are not taken in by it.

We tend to think that we have to fight off delusion in order to live in enlightenment. Or we imagine that if we can acquire enlightenment, we'll drive delusion away forever.

This is all only more delusion. We don't acquire enlightenment. We already have it. Or, more accurately, we're already in it. We're already of it. We can't be separated from it. All we have to do is to *see* that this is so, and freedom is there.

The ninth-century Zen teacher Linji (Rinzai, in Japanese), one of the great Zen teachers from China, said this about freedom:

> There are Zen students who are in chains when they go to
> a teacher, and the teacher adds another chain. The students
> are delighted, unable to discern one thing from another.
> This is called a guest looking at a guest.

Many of us come to Zen teachers wrapped in the chains of our concepts and ideas, expecting that the teacher will give us more of the same. This is why we're delighted when we meet a teacher who will hand us something. "Thank you very much," we say with heartfelt appreciation.

But it's just another thing for us to grasp—and we're used to grasping. We don't easily tolerate Zen teachers who make baffling and seemingly cryptic statements we can't understand. No, it's much more comfortable when they hand us something we can take hold of, sink our teeth into, carry with us, identify with, and call our own.

In our delusion, we think that awakening to *this moment* is just another item to complete and knock off our list of things to do. And so we try to get a better idea of what Reality is like—instead of stepping away from intellection altogether.

Zen teaching points to something quite subtle about *this moment*. What there is to *see* in *this moment* has the power to liberate us, though it's nothing you can grasp, nothing you can get hold of, nothing you can even have ideas about.

If you feel like you're getting something out of Zen, this is ordinary stuff. It's bondage, not freedom. There's nothing to get. You're just acquiring one more chain, one more item that keeps you bound, keeps you dissatisfied and looking around for the next goody. It's what you've always suffered; it's nothing new. It's just like all the other chains you're wearing, though it's of a different style, heft, material, and color. Like all the rest, you'll grow tired of it by and by.

There's nothing to figure out regarding enlightenment. It's not an explanation of Reality, so what's to figure out? Besides, that's what delusion is—figuring things out, putting everything into concepts.

Zen—that is, meditation—is simply coming back to *just this*—being present, noticing that we babble to ourselves, that we tell stories to ourselves, that we try to explain everything.

Zen will never say anything to you. If it does, it's only because *you're* making it up. If you tell yourself, "Oh, that was a good meditation. I really got into something deep there," it's nonsense. Pure delusion. And if you think, "Oh, my meditation was off, my mind was really disturbed," it's more delusion. Or, if you try to justify your meditation practice by saying, "My day goes so much better when it begins with meditation," it's all delusion. I never once heard my teacher talk like this. This is just our spinning minds jabbering to themselves.

Linji said, "This is called a guest looking at a guest." In other words, we attend, not to what we experience directly, but to what we make of it. Thus we ignore what in Zen we call the host—the actual experience of *this moment*. We ignore that there's no separation between Reality and ourselves.

Truth speaks to us directly, without words.

We're already in and of enlightenment, but we don't *see* it. Instead we go on thinking we're something separate and well defined—something with a name, an identity. If we'd only let such thoughts pass through, we'd realize we're already the host within the host—and all issues of bondage and freedom would slip away.

17

BEFORE IDEAS SPROUT

FOYAN, AN ANCIENT Chinese Zen teacher, observed, "You can be called a Zen student only when you perceive before signs appear, before falling into thought, before ideas sprout."

What's this about perceiving before signs appear? And what, exactly, are signs?

Signs are the marks by which we identify things—particularly when we give significance to those qualities. They are the concepts, descriptions, ideas, and values we attribute to things that give them reality in our minds.

Heat is a mark of fire. So are light and smoke. But a sign is something more. Signs contain meaning for us.

Yet signs are actually forms of delusion. We think they're indications of Reality, yet they are purely constructs of our own minds.

Thus all the myriad signs that appear are just our thoughts, our retelling and conceptualizing of what's actually experienced directly.

We cannot (and do not) experience Reality through signs. Reality occurs prior to our falling into thought, prior to our getting ideas, prior to our coming up with explanations. Reality is *before* things form in our minds as crystallized objects, one thing distinguished from another.

Foyan also said, "Zen practice requires nonattachment to thought." Here Foyan is not asking us to stop thinking. Instead, he is urging us not to take our thought objects as Reality. Instead of getting caught up in them, we can simply stop imagining that they have any substantiality.

Foyan echoes the *Diamond Sutra*, which says that the Buddha cannot be recognized by marks or signs. The word, however, the *Diamond Sutra* uses for Buddha is *Tathagata*, a compound Sanskrit word that means "coming and going, *thus*"—that is, coming and going in such a way that nothing actually comes or goes. *Tathagata*, as it's used here, is a metaphor for Reality—for immediate, direct experience. Tathagata is a description of how things are, which, as the term indicates, is no way in particular, since all is continuous, thoroughgoing flux. It points to actual experience, to what's perceived before things sprout in the mind, before we fall into thought, before signs appear.

The task of *this moment*, the issue at hand, is to pay attention to *this, right here*—to what's actually going on *before* we make anything of it. It's to realize how the mind conjures up endless ephemeral worlds and that if we would just look at these carefully, they would dissipate like smoke or mist—and we would wake up.

Unfortunately, most of us don't allow our cherished thoughts —our beliefs, our hatreds, our infatuations, our opinions, our calculations, our obsessions, our joys, our sorrows—to dissipate. In fact, we don't even notice that they *can* dissipate because we're so earnestly hanging on to them. We don't even notice that they're only thought.

Without realizing it, we hang on most dearly to what causes us the most grief and pain. At the same time, we reject freedom, fearing that somehow we'll lose something valuable in the process.

"Zen practice requires nonattachment to thought." You can be nonattached to thought only if you realize that your thought objects are not Real—that they're little more than objects in a dream.

Foyan reminds us that the thoughts and signs we conjure up are not the Real world. They're only models of the world and cannot substitute for Reality. Thus he's pointing out that our mind objects, including our sense of self and our sense of "the world, out there," are precisely what are *not* Real.

This is another way of presenting the Buddha's *anatta* teaching—the teaching that all things are without self.

This has to be *seen*. And it can only be *seen* directly—rather than explained or grasped—because it's not merely an idea but rather actual experience.

The issue in Zen, as in Buddhism in general, is Awareness. We need to *see* what's actually going on rather than focus on what we think.

We do not have to be confused about actual experience. We do not have to be tossed about by our emotions, our thoughts, our preferences. We can—and surely will—have thoughts and feelings, but they don't have to rule and ruin us.

Zen practice is attending to *this moment, seeing* it for what it is, which is nothing in particular, nothing graspable. And one of the easiest ways to spot when you're getting sidetracked is simply to watch the leaning of your own mind—when you incline either toward some object of desire or away from some object of aversion.

How do you stop your mind from leaning? Certainly not by making a direct effort to do so. This would be like trying to stop yourself from thinking of an elephant. You have to conjure up an elephant to make sure you're not thinking of one. It can't be done. You can't apply your will to make your mind straighten up because the very application of will is itself an inclination of your mind.

Instead, it's enough to simply notice that your mind is leaning. To the extent that you're aware it's leaning, it straightens up on its own.

Getting caught up in signs, falling into thought, chasing ideas when they sprout—these are all leanings of mind. As the mind straightens up, these states of mind all fall away naturally. What's left is what's been *here* all along: Reality. It's only a matter of *seeing*.

18

TRUE FREEDOM

Another Chinese Zen teacher from ancient times, Ying-an, told his students, "When you pass through, no one can pin you down, no one can call you back."

We might get the idea from this that in Zen there's some barrier, some goal, some threshold you must come up to and then cross over or pass through. And once you get through, the wonderful, delicious freedom of enlightenment is yours. At that point you've made it. You're happy and serene. You're untouchable and invincible. Nobody can tell you what to do, and no one can call you back. You're really free.

But if we look at what Ying-an said in this way, we don't understand him at all. In fact, we're dead wrong on all counts. This misunderstanding comes from using our ordinary, ego-centered perspective, which is precisely what Ying-an is helping us drop.

We're very confused about this issue of freedom. We think it means something like, "I can do what I want. No one can tell me what to do. There are no restrictions anymore. It's totally up to me." But notice that there's an adolescent ring to such thoughts.

I once saw several teenagers interviewed on a TV report about marketing tobacco to youth. A reporter asked a group of teenagers, "Are you smoking because your parents don't approve of it?" Several of them said yes, and one added, "They tell us not to do something, man, and we're going to do it."

To many of us grown-ups, this remains our idea of freedom, though we might express it in regard to religion, career, or civic duties. But from a Buddhist perspective, "you can't tell me what to do" is an expression of bondage, not freedom.

Because the Buddha said, "What I call liberation, the world calls resignation," some people view Buddhism as giving in to or giving up something—as if these teachings recommend that we lie down like a doormat rather than stand up and face Reality. People suffering from this form of delusion may say, "All those forces out there are immense. Stop trying to fight them. Just surrender yourself totally; then you'll experience enlightenment or freedom."

But this is not *at all* what the Buddha spoke of as liberation. In fact, this very thinking is bondage itself. It's still our ordinary, self-oriented state of mind.

The reason the Buddha's message sounds like resignation to us is because we still presume a self "here" and something else "out there." But the Buddha pointed out that there isn't any world "out there" apart from you. That is, true separation between you and other things simply cannot be found. Liberation comes not from knuckling under to the rules of the universe but from *seeing* that there's no separate person to give in and no separate, overwhelming universe to give in to.

What the Buddha is talking about is the experience you're having *right now*. If you'll look at it for a moment, you'll *see* it's immediate, continuous, and inseparable from something else "out there."

You see and hear a car through the window, and you think, "A car is out there on the street." But where is the sound? Is it "out there" on the street? Is it in your ear? Is it in your brain? Is it in the vibration of the air between you "here" and the street "out there"? Where are all these events taking place?

Most of us think, "There's something out there, and I'm in here. I am separate from all of that out there." Precisely *because* we think in this way, we're jerked around by the world— or, more accurately, by our thoughts and feelings about it. These place us and keep us in bondage.

But if we *see* deeply and carefully what our actual experience is, we can realize that there's no "us" apart from "all that, out there." This *seeing* is what Ying-an called "passing through."

When Ying-an says, "no one will pin you down, no one will call you back," he's acknowledging that there's nothing to pin down or call back. There never was and never will be. Just as we can't actually place "that sound, outside" anywhere, nothing has actually formed anywhere. If we investigate our direct experience, we'll discover that we can't pin *anything* down, ever—including what we think of as ourselves.

Once *this moment* is *seen* for what it is, there's no more believing in a universe consisting of a tiny, isolated "you" that is distantly viewing everything "out there." There's no more need to protect and defend yourself against "out there" or to get, earn, or coax good things from it.

This is liberation, enlightenment, freedom of mind. It's the very opposite of resignation; it's the dissolution of the desire to get everything you want or to do whatever you please.

You already have the capacity to *see* Truth *right now.* You don't (and can't) get this capacity from another—not from me, from this book, from Buddha, or from anything or anyone else. How could you possibly get what you already have?

No one can pin you down; no one can call you back. Just as no one binds you, no one blinds you.

19

MISGUIDED
MEDITATION

WHEN WE BEGIN a regular meditation practice, we often assume that we know what meditation is. This seems reasonable enough. After all, we've had instruction in it and perhaps taken a course in it. We do it every day. Why shouldn't we know what meditation is?

Yet it usually takes time before we really understand what we're doing in meditation. In my own case, for example, I had been "meditating," at least outwardly, for many years before I began to understand what I was doing.

In fact, it wasn't until I met a good Zen teacher that this began to clear up for me. At first, my teacher would say things about meditation that really threw me. He'd call it useless and remind me that it wouldn't get me anywhere. Yet he'd sit in meditation every day, sometimes for hours.

But he wasn't trying to be clever or creative or even meta-phorical. He was being completely straightforward, precise, and accurate—even literal, though it took me some time to realize it.

One of the biggest snares we lay for ourselves in Zen is that we refer to meditation as "sitting." This is quite misleading. It implies (and reinforces in our minds) that meditation has something to do with being seated.

In part this is because the Japanese word we use for meditation is *zazen*, which literally means "sitting meditation." In part it's because another Japanese word we use for meditation, *shikantaza*, is commonly translated as "just sitting."

But we miss the essential point here, which is the "just" part. *Just doing the dishes. Just playing basketball. Just driving. Just seeing. Just sitting.* All of these are genuine meditation. I mean this quite literally. Indeed, the great Zen teacher Dogen echoed this when he wrote that *sanzen*—meditation in its fullest expression—"has nothing whatever to do with sitting or lying down."

Meditation can occur anywhere. You don't have to run for a cushion. (In fact, at many Zen centers, it's usual for people to practice meditation while working, walking, or eating as well as while sitting.) Meditation is simply collecting the mind. While driving a car, you can collect the mind. In a conversation with your boss, you can collect the mind. While preparing an apple pie or writing a letter, you can collect the mind.

It doesn't matter what the activity is. If you really understand meditation, it can reach into every activity of your life, 24/7.

It's not that we can, or even ought to be, fully present 24/7. I have yet to meet anyone who can do that. I certainly can't. But this is not the point. The point is, whenever you notice that your attention is shifting away from *here* and *now*, bring it back. And when your mind checks out again, bring it back. It's off again. Just come back. You can do this anywhere.

In Zen we call this meditation *practice*, because that's what we're doing: practicing the single-pointed activity of returning to *this moment*, breath by breath, day after day.

This is not easy to do. Most of the time there's a lot of distraction in our lives. Of course, much of the time we invite much of this distraction. We even try to imitate our machines and multitask, thinking there's virtue in it. But this sort of activity actually disperses the mind. Meditation is just the opposite.

People often think that the amount of time you spend in formal sitting meditation is what's most important, but this is not the case. Rather, the three most important elements to remember in taking up a meditation practice are:

1. Do it with regularity

2. Do it with others, and

3. Refrain from judgment about how you're doing.

There's no point in taking up a practice of meditation if you're only going to do it every now and then, when the mood strikes you. This is like trying to cook potatoes by putting them in a pot of water on the stove and turning the burner on high for a few seconds every hour or so.

Regularity in formal sitting meditation is essential. This alone will cultivate an attitude and an approach to life that's invaluable. No matter what or how you feel about meditation, you do it at a set, predetermined time as opposed to at whim or on the spur of the moment. When it's time for formal meditation, just meditate, regardless of whether you want to or not.

If at all possible, meditating with others is also very good, particularly if you want to take up the practice for the long run. Others will give you encouragement as you, in turn, offer encouragement to others. Meditating with others will also help keep you from drifting off into your own peculiar mental space.

Finally, it's impossible to be present when your mind is full of judgment. In meditation, gradually we learn to just be *here* without a lot of comment about what's going on. (Whatever we would say is just our delusion, anyway.) First we can learn to avoid judging our meditation. "Oh, that was a deep one!" Or, "I can't do this right. I'm no good at it." As we learn not to judge ourselves, we can learn not to judge others as well. To the extent we judge we don't *just see*.

When we practice formal sitting meditation, we pare back our activity until we're not engaged in anything except sitting and breathing. This won't last, of course. Sooner or later, thinking creeps into our activity, no matter what we do. That's okay. Even as you sit quietly, doing nothing, the mind will

keep coughing up stuff. This is nothing to be alarmed about.
It's normal. Just don't get caught up with the thinking. Just
let it go.

What if this time you *can't* let it go? That's okay, too. It will
go on its own—if you let it.

Eventually we learn that we don't have to participate in
what the mind picks up. We learn that we don't have to create
and perpetuate suffering and discontent. We discover that it's
possible for us to *see* and *know* true freedom.

20

TURNING THINGS AROUND

We've all tasted the kicking and screaming mind. Inwardly, all of us kick and scream about things that don't please us. There's something we want that we're not getting. Or else what we don't want keeps coming our way. We don't want *this;* we want that. But the world just keeps dishing up *this* for us.

Sometimes we can manage to find things to distract such a mind, to appease it, or even to please it. As a result, we devote a great deal of time and energy to these endeavors. Because we don't like our kicking and screaming mind, our usual approach is to try to change the world, thinking that this will make us feel better. We think and act as if, somehow, through the right planning, strategizing, and acting, we can eventually make everything just right or at least satisfactory. And then, we tell ourselves, our kicking and screaming mind will quiet down and we can at last be peaceful and happy.

But the simple fact that we live with others guarantees that things are not always going to go our way. Sooner or later we're going to come into conflict with others, and with the world, in various ways. No matter what we do, dissatisfaction will continue to come up—at least as long as we continue to think our problem is "out there."

The very fact that dissatisfaction inevitably shows up tells us something worth noting: that our problems are *not* "out there," in the world. No matter how large a fuss you make, the world—the natural world—doesn't care. Nor does the natural world kick and scream. It just goes on—dishing up this, dishing up that.

Zen practice is not merely about learning to let go of this discontented, noisy, complaining, kicking, screaming mind. It's about learning to forget about it. Whether such a mind lingers or not, we don't worry about it. We just let it go. We turn our attention from the entanglements we conjure up in our mind to what's actually going on, *right here, right now,* in this moment.

In formal sitting meditation, because there isn't much going on—since we've limited our behavior, our speech, and the space we occupy—we can now, voluntarily, face and observe this mind that wants to be pleased all the time. When we're in meditation, the mind that *doesn't* want to be anxious, angry, displeased, or discontented can come forth.

On the other hand, if dissatisfaction is festering in your mind, sitting quietly in meditation will bring it out in stark relief. This provides a wonderful opportunity: by bringing this dissatisfaction up and facing it, by looking at it and *seeing* what's going on, you can let go of your kicking and screaming mind.

Let's look more closely at this matter of our discontent—our wanting things to be other than the way they are.

We live in a culture in which we're expected to spend a great deal of time trying to please ourselves in various ways. Yet it's this very rushing to please ourselves that underlies our displeasure, unhappiness, and misery.

We need to bring our ego out front and take a good, hard look at it. When we live out of our "I want it this way" or "I don't want it that way" mind, our immediate experience is dissatisfaction, misery, pain, suffering, obsession, desperation, frustration, anger, and so on. This ego, this "me," this center of everything, wants (and often demands) to be pleased and protected. This is where all our suffering resides and from where all our difficulties stem.

For all its concern with pleasing itself, our ego is its own worst enemy. But if we're attentive, we know what to look for, and if we're entirely honest with ourselves, we'll *see* the ego's game for what it is and not be taken in by it. This *seeing* gives us an opportunity to turn things around—to find a different kind of mind.

When I was studying with Katagiri Roshi, we acquired a new bell for the meditation hall. We soon discovered that we could more easily produce a good sound by tilting the bell. Though the bell no longer sat stably on its cushion, we got what we wanted out of it—a good sound without much effort.

When our teacher saw this, however, he immediately leveled the bell. "Don't force the bell to accommodate you," he said. "You learn to accommodate the bell."

When, moment by moment, we recreate ourselves to fit the demands of the occasion, we'll not experience a kicking and screaming mind. Whatever the world dishes up, we take it on—not on our own terms but on the world's. On behalf of the Whole, we forget ourselves and our delusion.

An ancient Zen teacher said, "The Way is always with people, but people themselves chase after things."

The Way—Truth, Reality, enlightenment—is always with people. It's with you *now*. It's not something "out there" that you have to run after—that you have to fix or possess. Realize that running after, and running from, is your problem. Realize that the Way is not like that. It's always with you.

If you don't bear this in mind, you'll not understand, and you'll just go running off once again. You'll go trying to acquire or possess Zen, and you'll treat it in the same way you treat everything else that you go after.

Look at the two people above. Outwardly, they look very much the same, but inwardly they are utterly different.

The person on the left has a noisy mind, a grasping mind, and is filled with notions and techniques. Not so for the person on the right, who is not busy with any notion or technique.

The person on the left sits to become enlightened—to become a buddha. The one on the right is sitting *as* a buddha.

The person on the left has a mind full of explanations, justifications, and reasons for practicing sitting meditation. The one on the right is *just sitting*.

The person on the left doesn't yet understand the one on the right but presumes that they're both doing exactly the same thing. The person on the left doesn't yet understand that freedom of mind is immediate and comes with understanding, not with going through all the "correct" motions. (The proper motions follow, they don't lead. And, yes, we must nevertheless go through the motions.)

The person on the left doesn't understand that they can't go after what they think they're going after. (In fact they really don't know what they're going after; they're just holding to an idea of enlightenment.) The person on the right, on the other hand, has no reason to do what they're doing; that's why they do it so completely. It's also why they *know* true wisdom and compassion, and complete peace and freedom of mind.

The fact that we already have what we would awaken to—Truth, Reality—is precisely how and why we can awaken to it. It's not something that can appear to us given the right technique or circumstances. It's always *here;* it's always with us. It's always with you—or, rather, you're always with It.

What's being said here is so utterly simple that you're likely to miss it. Yet if you look with an honest eye, you can *see* it.

The way to be totally free from displeasure, from dissatisfaction, from longing, from loathing, from the kicking and screaming mind, is right *here*.

21

IT'S ENOUGH
TO BE AWAKE

THERE'S A STORY of a Zen teacher named Kuei-shan, from ninth-century China, and his student, Yang-shan. Yang-shan came to Kuei-shan and asked, "When the ten thousand things come up to you, what should you do?"

Kuei-shan said, "Green is not yellow; long is not short. Each thing manages its own; why should I interfere?"

Unfortunately, most of us think we need to interfere. We feel we have to do something, we have to be something, we have to arrange something. We think that if we can arrange things in the proper way, everything will be okay.

What we don't recognize is that the very things we try to arrange are imaginary, frozen, mentally packaged up—while Reality is thoroughgoing flux and flow.

We carry on as though our lives can be properly arranged for our happiness if only we can somehow master the art of arranging. Once we attain this mastery, we can get what we want. We can be satisfied. We can make our lives work. We can make the rest of the world work.

Yet we never manage to make the world or our life into what we want it to be—at least not for long. Things change, and so we try something else. We start to think again about what would improve our lot, and the whole delusion cycles through once more.

If we scrutinize it carefully, we'll *see* dissatisfaction woven right into the heart of this approach to life. And we might also notice that our situation is perfectly fine *before* we step in and try to improve it.

But aren't we better off today in all kinds of ways than we were in times past?

In trying to prove or decide that we're better off—or that we're not better off—we're yet again grasping for an explanation or an answer. But whatever we take hold of, it's dubious from the start.

When we say, "we're better off," we're imagining that somehow the story is over and we've reached a point of stasis. But such a point never happens in real life. Indeed, part of what characterizes fairy tales is that they end at a momentarily happy point, or else they pretend that things will stay that way eternally ("and they lived happily ever after").

But in Reality the story is never over. There's just ongoing flux and flow. So how can we say we're better off? It's an absurd thought. No one knows how the story is going to unfold. No matter what we would point to, it can always be countered. It never stops.

Nevertheless, we act and plan as though there are actual endings. This is because, in our delusion, we ignore thorough-going change, believing that things actually endure and persist, even if only for a moment. It's all an illusion, but we don't *see* it for what it is.

There's another story of Master Kuei-shan, in which he said to his monks, "Today the weather is cold—as cold as it was a year ago. And next year we'll have the same cold weather." Turning to Yang-shan, he said, "Tell me, what are the days of the year repeating?"

Yang-shan, who was a senior monk, made a gesture of respect but said nothing.

Kuei-shan said, "I knew you couldn't say anything." Then he looked at Hsiang-yen, one of his junior monks, and said, "What about you?"

"I think I can say something about that," Hsiang-yen began.

"I'm glad that the senior monk could not answer me," interrupted Kuei-shan.

What can we truly say about ongoing, cyclical, ever-changing existence? The moment we try to say something about it—the moment we try to put it into a frozen, conceptual form—we step away from the actual Reality we find ourselves in.

The awakened only want to be awake. They don't want to be deceived about what is going on. This is enough.

One of the Buddha's great insights speaks directly to this matter of stepping into the world with an agenda, with a program, with the idea that Reality must be directed in a certain way. He recognized all this as the reification of a mentally constructed illusion called "me" and that today we often call the ego. When we buy into this illusion, we create a different kind of activity than is found naturally in the world. It's intentional activity—that is, activity motivated by the part, activity initiated by a self—as opposed to activity that comes out of Reality as a Whole. In other words, it's point-like as opposed to being field-like. And because it doesn't take the Whole into account, the result is *dukkha*—dissatisfaction, frustration, vexation, grief, sorrow, fear, loathing, confusion, and lamentation.

This doesn't mean that we shouldn't act. It's impossible not to act. We're part of the world, and the world is constantly acting. Indeed, it's nothing *but* activity, motion, energy. Nothing stays put for an instant. Even if we choose inaction, that's still action because *everything* is acting. Even if we sit motionless in a stream, we still interact with everything that passes by.

The awakened *see* that the big question in life is not "What do I do to arrange the world to my satisfaction?" but "How do I learn to attend to what's going on?" In other words, our question has become a true interest in awakening rather than a desire to acquire something or to please ourselves in some egoistic way.

When we learn to attend to what's actually happening and *see* things as they are, action still occurs, but it's no longer driven or guided by personal desire or design.

In every moment we step into a new situation. Usually we have a plan or agenda for it. It's not wrong to have a plan, but it's far more urgent that we keep our eyes open in each moment and *see* what's happening *now*. And sometimes, since nothing's standing still, our plan may become a hindrance, especially if we're attached to it. And if we're not paying attention to what's actually going on, we'll not *see* all the possibilities that constantly unfold.

To act or not act is not the real question. For the awakened, what comes first is simply being awake—*seeing* what's going on. And in *seeing* what's going on in *this moment*, appropriate—that is, natural—action can occur.

Kuei-shan said, "Why interfere?" When we act out of *seeing*, we are no longer interfering with the world; instead, we are operating the way the natural world operates—out of the Whole, out of Totality.

For the awakened the primary concern is simply to *see* what is taking place and to act in accord with it.

This is how the awakened differ from those of us who are caught up in delusion. It's a very subtle, quiet, and gentle point, but its implications are total. Realizing this creates a complete transformation of heart and mind.

Enlightenment is nothing more than this: to be fully present, to *see* the grasping nature of our own minds, and not to act out of that grasping. It's to *see* ourselves not as separate, not as lacking, not as in charge, not as weak and helpless.

When we're no longer acting out of a sense of self—out of our wants, our fears, our worries, our obsessions—we're no longer being driven by the compulsion to arrange everything in a way that feels comfortable and satisfying.

The truth is, you'll never succeed at getting things arranged just so. You'll never live happily ever after. You'll never please and protect yourself for more than a fleeting moment. In fact, if you look for it, you'll never even put your finger on just what it is that you're trying to please and protect. So why interfere?

If we look carefully at what's going on in each moment, we'll *see* there's nothing we need to take hold of—indeed, there's nothing we *can* take hold of.

All of this doesn't mean that we can't or shouldn't act. It doesn't mean we can't plan or think or believe or hold ideas. It *does* mean that we don't have to be deceived by this or taken in by that.

For the awakened, motivation has shifted. The motive now is simply to be awake from moment to moment and to deal with every fresh and new situation as it arises. We step into each situation not knowing but with our eyes open to what's actually taking place. We act from there. *Seeing* each new moment as it arises creates action that is in accord with how things are *now*.

The universe is reborn in each moment. You are reborn with it. Countless versions of "you" have come and gone since you've picked up this book—a new "you" is born in each moment. Nothing is persisting. So what "you" is there to please and protect?

For the awakened, there's only the intent to return to *this realization*, not to get caught up in the belief of persistence.

Many of us first come to Zen wanting to know what Reality is like. But once we've learned to look very carefully, we *see* that Reality can't possibly be *like* anything. It is, and has to be, itself.

As Sextus Empiricus, an ancient skeptic, observed, "For it is sufficient . . . to live by experience, and without subscribing to beliefs. . . ." We do not need to believe. We only need to *see*.

Just to be awake is enough—for any of us. Were we to awaken, we'd *see* that, all along, our purest and truest desire has only been to be awake.

22

LIFE WITHOUT MEASURE

Zen is about doing your best. The problem is that we usually don't realize what doing our best is.

Instead, we get hold of some concept about *what it means* to do our best. We come up with ideas about what's good and what's bad and what we should and shouldn't be doing. And then we set goals and standards against which we measure our progress.

In doing so, we take everything into the territory of ego. "*I* will do my best." "*I* will succeed." "*I* will do better than others." We get caught up in thought and personal ambition, even when it comes to meditation or wisdom or compassion. "*I* will realize selflessness." "*I* will attain Nirvana." It's ridiculous.

Look at the state of mind we create by such thoughts. It's our usual greedy, grasping, acquiring mind. It's fragmented and agitated.

In Zen, doing your best is about cultivating a mind that doesn't get caught up in egoistic practices. It's watching for speech and behavior that set us apart, cut us off, or put us in opposition to others.

Ryokan, a Japanese Zen monk and poet who lived from 1758 to 1831, had a true Zen mind. There are many stories about Ryokan—and some stories have multiple variations—but here are two that beautifully demonstrate this mind.

One day when Ryokan was away, a thief went into his hut looking for something to steal. Finding nothing of value inside, the disappointed thief was about to leave when Ryokan showed up.

Taking pity on the thief, Ryokan offered him his clothes. The bewildered thief took them and made off.

That evening, as Ryokan sat naked outside his grass hut, he watched the full moon rise. "Poor fellow," he thought, "I wish I could give him this moon."

While the moon can certainly be taken literally here, it also helps to know that in Zen the full moon is a symbol for enlightenment. But while Ryokan may have wished he could give the poor fellow a mind of enlightenment, of course he couldn't. We have to cultivate that mind within ourselves. No one can do it for us.

In another story, Ryokan was sitting in his hut when he noticed a bamboo shoot sprouting from the dirt floor under his veranda. He left it alone and it continued to grow. In time, it reached the ceiling. At that point, Ryokan opened a hole in the roof so the bamboo could continue to grow.

Doing your best is coming into *this moment* and *seeing* what's actually going on. It's realizing that your life is not your own—that in fact you live inseparably from the Whole.

Most of us live believing we're separate beings. This only breeds loneliness, selfishness, pain, and difficulty. Still, because we see ourselves in this way—and because we try to assuage the ache we feel from living this way—we expend enormous energy and resources to alter ourselves, each other, and our environment, all in an effort to suit our immediate concerns. Meanwhile, we have little or no awareness of how our actions affect others—and little recognition that what affects others affects us as well.

It's very easy for us to look "out there" and react to how "that" adversely affects "me." "I don't want bamboo growing there!" "I don't want bees nesting under my eaves." "I don't want my investments to return less than 10 percent." Yet we rarely consider the quality of our minds or the impact of our actions on the world.

Consider the practice of meditation. Generally we think of it as sitting in a particular way for a designated period of time. But that's a narrow definition. A more complete and accurate definition is simply being present with what's actually taking place rather than with our intellectual and emotional readouts— the explanations, justifications, rationalizations, and worries that so often override and usurp our attention. Meditation is thus incompatible with our business-as-usual mind, our mind of wanting to manipulate and control.

Nevertheless, the mind of meditation is a mind that we can find anytime, anywhere. Even with a busy schedule, we can find this mind that's attentive and ready, that's not attached to any particular outcome, that doesn't insist that things go a particular way. Meditation is always about what's going on *right now*, no matter what it happens to be—driving the car, having a conversation, lying in bed.

One of the most common questions I receive when I give meditation instruction is, "How much should I meditate?" It's not an unreasonable question, and there's nothing wrong with it. But it reflects our usual approach and expectations.

What's important is not how much meditation you do but the regularity and the spirit with which you do it. If you take it up wholeheartedly and regularly, you'll begin to cultivate the mind I'm speaking of.

So don't worry about how much you should do this practice. Being present isn't based on the amount of time you force yourself to sit on the cushion. In fact, if you look for a moment at the very attitude and approach that says "more is better," you'll see it's a greedy, grasping, fragmented mind, not an integrated one.

In Zen practice we simply attend to *right now*, to *this moment*—without concern for making the mind better or more focused or more concentrated or enlightened.

It's not a matter of trying to wrestle our mind into submission or forcing ourselves to sit on a cushion. (Actually, many of us start out this way, but sooner or later this approach has got to end, either with realization or with giving up.)

To do our best, we only need to realize that our usual approach is inappropriate and to change our attitude regarding this practice. We have to learn to *just practice*—wholeheartedly, with no goal, for no gain or reason.

Our natural state of mind—the natural, pure quality of mind—is already present. We don't have to "get it." Enlightenment is already present. It's not something we have to acquire.

In Zen our practice is to come into *this moment,* to be fully alive in each moment, to be reborn in each moment, again and again—fresh, new, vibrant, alive, clean, and healthy. It's to live naturally and without blame.

To the extent that we live in *this moment*—completely burn ourselves up in *this moment,* with no residue—we live with a free mind. At the same time, we also free others by allowing them to live their lives undisturbed. And to the extent that we awaken to past wrongs we may have done to others, we're free to forgive ourselves and make amends.

Thus we can live a life of sanity, peace, and harmony. Thus we do our best.

23

THE MOST VALUABLE THING
IN THE WORLD

A STUDENT WENT to the Zen teacher Ts'ao-shan and asked, "What is the most valuable thing in the world?" Ts'ao-shan replied, "The head of a dead cat."

"Why is the head of a dead cat the most valuable thing in the world?" asked the student.

"Because no one can name its price," said Ts'ao-shan.

Woe to those of us who *do* know the price of things, for we go through life evaluating everything. We put everything and every event on some kind of scale. "How good is it?" "What's it good for?" "What can I get out of this?" "What's in it for me?"

At the same time we do all this, we're miserable, unhappy, wanting, greedy, begging, scheming. We're dissatisfied yet have no clue about what our problem is. We see no connection between our endless evaluating and our recurring unhappiness. And so, already, we're reaching for the next thing and then the next and the next and the next. Meanwhile, we miss the most valuable thing in life. Over and over again, we keep making the same mistake.

What we really want out of life is not something that can be obtained in this way. It's not a commodity that can be bought and sold. (For that matter, it's not even an "it.")

The most valuable thing in life (which, incidentally, is not literally the head of a dead cat) is very simple. That's why we miss it so easily. Nevertheless, it's always at hand.

What we really want—and what is truly priceless—is to wake up. We want to *see*. But there isn't any particular thing to *see*—as if you could grab it or hatch it or put its pieces together. It's not a physical item you can hold in your hand. It's not a mental object you can hold in your mind, either.

The things we can put price tags on—or measure in any other way—are precisely *not* the things our heart sings for, the things we truly, deeply need and want.

What we truly, deeply need and want we already have—and it's truly priceless. And it's precisely because it's priceless that we tend not to *see* it. We're too distracted by all the things we *do* evaluate. We assume that the most valuable thing in the world *must* look like all the other things we habitually evaluate—only bigger or deeper or prettier or more moving.

So what is this most precious thing? It's not a thing at all. It's *this very moment*.

In *Zen Mind, Beginner's Mind*, Shunryu Suzuki writes, "When my talk is over, your listening is over. There is no need to remember what I say; there is no need to understand what I say." And, I would add, there's no need to take hold of what is said.

You don't have to listen to a talk or read a book (including this one) with an attitude that puts a price tag on it at the end. On the one hand, it seems natural and sensible to want it to be worth your time and effort so that you come away from it with something. But we err in imagining that this "something" should (or can) be tangible enough to put in our pocket.

What's of Real value is not tangible at all. We already *know* this, though we're usually looking the other way.

When listening to a talk or reading a book—particularly one such as this—it isn't important what you walk away with. It doesn't matter whether you can repeat or remember what you read. What's important—what's priceless—is transformation of mind.

When we encounter the experience of the moment—whether listening to a lecture or sitting on a fishing dock, watching a bobber in the water—the most valuable thing is to be fully present, engaged in the moment, truly alive. If we do this, then as we walk away from "that moment" (as we necessarily must), we can stay with *just this*—with what's going on *now*.

It isn't a matter of getting the right idea of it so that we can put it into practice later on. It isn't a matter of acquiring something we can use. It isn't a matter of anything but *just this*.

You already have full understanding. Only remember not to grasp, not to say, "I've got it." (Whenever we think or say, "I've got it," that's delusion.)

. . .

I recently read of a company that has managed to breed seeds that won't reproduce themselves. When farmers buy this seed and plant their fields with it, if the weather cooperates it will produce a good yield, which the farmer can then sell on the market.

But if the farmer decides to take a portion of the seed from that crop to use in planting next year, those seeds won't sprout. This is because the seed was genetically engineered to produce seeds that won't germinate. In other words, humans have altered seed—the very symbol of fertility, regeneration, and life—to defy a basic characteristic of life: the ability to reproduce.

This kind of action comes out of a mind that puts a value on everything, even the fundamental characteristics of life. This mind wants things to be valuable. It doesn't want anything for what it is; it wants things for what they can bring us.

When we live based on such a mind, we don't want Reality. Instead, we want abstractions. Thus we lose sight of how we actually live in this world.

This kind of action the Buddha referred to as "willed action" *(karma)*, and it's radically different from natural or unwilled action. It's action that doesn't take into account the Whole. It ignores the actual fabric in which everything occurs.

In contrast, looking at the Whole picture doesn't give us anything we can quantify or evaluate or put a price tag on. Thus we can *see* for ourselves that there's no way to truly satisfy ourselves by pricing, measuring, or evaluating everything. We can't say what's intrinsically good or bad or valuable or worthless. It's simply *this*—or, more precisely, Awareness of *this*—that is most valuable. Yet we can *see* that any attempt to name its price is absurd.

24

BEFORE WE SAY

"Who, Subhuti, will grasp this perfect wisdom as here explained?"

Thereupon the Venerable Ananda said: "Those who cannot fall back will grasp it, or persons who have reached sound views. . . ."

"No one," said Subhuti, "will grasp this perfect wisdom as here explained. For nothing at all has been indicated, lit up, or communicated. So there will be no one who can grasp it."

—from *The Perfection of Wisdom in Eight Thousand Lines*

BEFORE THE FACT, wise people often look like fools. In contrast, experts often look like fools afterward.

To give an example, in the mid-1980s the Soviet power plant at Chernobyl exploded, spewing radioactive materials around the globe. (The level of radioactive iodine that fell with the rain in Minnesota a few days later was 48 times higher than normal.) Less than a year before this event, a high Soviet deputy minister assured us that nuclear power plants were safe. He specifically mentioned the Chernobyl plant, saying that it would be ten thousand years before there'd be an accident of any consequence.

Only a few months before the space shuttle *Challenger* blew up, a NASA official assured us that there would be tens of thousands of launches before there would be any explosion of a space vehicle upon launch. And yet already, tragically, we've seen a second catastrophic failure of a space shuttle—though this time on reentry, which is considered by experts to be far less risky than launch.

Not long ago, experts assured us that we're all safe from bioterrorism. Since then, however, we've seen a number of deaths from anthrax and major disruptions to our postal service because of anthrax being sent through the mail. Our officials have since ordered 300 million doses of smallpox vaccine.

In all of these cases, and many others, people supposedly in the know have either overlooked or ignored what is obvious to anyone who could *just see*. Furthermore, it's becoming increasingly apparent that such gaps in vision are becoming ever more perilous.

Yet this is the very nature of knowing, as we commonly understand knowing. For in holding and maintaining a particular view, even if we become an expert, we must necessarily leave some things out of that view or ignore them altogether. There's no allowance for wisdom—for with wisdom (as with Reality), nothing is held or maintained and nothing is left out.

Once we had leaders who sought the advice of wise people; today our leaders rely primarily on experts. This is understandable for two reasons: (1) experts are easier to identify and certify, and (2) wise people don't advertise themselves as such.

The problem is not that experts don't fulfill vital functions. They often do. It's just that experts don't direct our attention to Reality, Truth, or the Whole. Because their knowledge is confined to a limited sphere, they can do nothing to bring us to where we can *see* what's really going on. In fact, they inadvertently turn our minds from it.

A requirement for becoming an expert is that you must put boundaries around the territory you study. Thus experts have their own private, internally consistent arguments, which they put forth in language that often only other experts or aspiring experts in the field can speak. In addition, what experts say is usually consistent, clear, and above all nonparadoxical (and thus, we assume, true). But because they've managed to keep it all inside a limited sphere, what they conclude inevitably fails to take into account unbounded, free-flowing Truth and Reality.

In other words, whatever conceptual model we come up with, it cannot ultimately serve as a substitute for Reality. And while we might be tempted to shrug off this observation, ignoring its implications is potentially devastating.

When we confine ourselves to a bubble, a cocoon, a limited sphere, it's difficult for us to see that *all* our conceptual knowledge floats on the surface of the vast sea of Reality, which contains a myriad of other bubbles. And from inside any bubble, it's hard to realize that Truth is *seen* only when our bubble breaks.

Yet each such bubble surely will break, sooner or later. And when it does, we would do well not to give in to the urge to scramble immediately into yet another bubble.

It is best if we break our bubbles ourselves. But this can't be done by scheming, planning, or trying to do so. It can be accomplished only through *seeing*.

What the awakened *see* is Reality—Truth—before anything is made of it. What they have to say regarding this *seeing* is called Dharma—with a capital *D*.

Dharma can't be solidified or conceptualized. It can't be captured in a particular phrase or word; it can't be laid out in a theory, a diagram, or a book—including this one.

Thus any teaching that points to Truth must ultimately erase itself. And in erasing itself, such teaching—Dharma—is necessarily self-referential. (I often liken it to someone writing on a chalkboard with the right hand while the left hand follows, erasing what has been written.) As a result, it may appear paradoxical or contradictory. Yet it is not.

Unlike ordinary teaching, which presents itself as enduring and useful, Dharma teachings are offered with the understanding that they will pass away—that they have only provisional, temporary use. The Buddha, for example, likened his teaching to a raft used to cross a river. Once it has served its purpose—once the river has been crossed—it's best to leave the raft behind or it will become an unnecessary burden.

Unfortunately, many of us dismiss the self-referential nature of such teachings as soon as we encounter them. We simply think, "But it's a time-honored teaching! Why would I want to get rid of it? That doesn't make sense!" Thus we turn our heads from teachings that point directly to Truth without a second thought and take up views we can more easily grasp and hold on to. We're not used to *just seeing*.

When we dismiss Dharma, however, it means that we have not yet noticed that it's actually our concepts that don't match Reality—ever. We also don't *see* that it's our very desire to avoid paradox, self-reference, self-retraction (stepping away from what we've formulated in our minds), and inconceivability that obstructs us from *seeing* Truth, or Reality.

Unlike Dharma, ordinary teachings don't admit or account for paradox or thoroughgoing change. Rather, they try to pin down their subjects, to make them appear sound and solid. But any teaching that presents itself in this way—whether it's about politics, economics, psychology, religion, science, or auto mechanics—is an attempt to embalm something that will inevitably pass away.

When we believe that what we conceive of or describe is what's really going on—when we believe that we actually can take hold of Truth—our knowledge is faulty. Truth simply can't be described, modeled, or represented. Yet it can be *seen*.

. . .

We want Truth badly, but we mistakenly look for it in concepts, in words, or in phrases. We act as though it were something we could stuff in our pockets and take out once in a while to show people.

Yet while we labor hard to promote and protect what we believe to be the dazzling beauty in our pocket, Truth continues to reveal to us nothing but constant flux—total relativity, thoroughgoing change.

When it comes to Dharma, there are no experts. You can't become an expert on Truth. You can't master your life.

You can, however, wake up.

25

NEEDLE IN THE WATER

KANADEVA, who would eventually become the fifteenth ancestor of Zen, came to see Nagarjuna, the fourteenth ancestor, hoping to become his student. Like Nagarjuna, Kanadeva had a reputation for being very wise, and also like Nagarjuna, he loved rhetoric, philosophy, and debate.

Nagarjuna was aware of this when Kanadeva came to call, and he thought, "Let's see how wise he is. I'll test him." And so Nagarjuna had a servant fill a bowl full of water to the brim and bring it out to Kanadeva as he approached the gate. Nagarjuna watched from a window to see what Kanadeva would do.

When the servant presented the full bowl of water to Kanadeva, Kanadeva took out a needle and put it in the water. Kanadeva then took the bowl and carried it to Nagarjuna, who was greatly pleased. The two of them laughed heartily. They had one mind and understood each other thoroughly.

Thereafter, Nagarjuna and Kanadeva taught together at times. They also traveled about together.

There are many interpretations of the bowl and the needle in which the bowl is said to be a symbol of X and the needle is a symbol of Y. For example, the bowl is sometimes said to symbolize realization or enlightenment and the needle the aspiration for awakening. But if we're not careful, we can easily get caught up in such images and not really digest this story. We need to dig deeper.

First of all, the bowl was completely full of clear, pure water. Kanadeva could see to the bottom, even though the bowl was full. It was an expression of Emptiness, of Totality.

Nagarjuna presented Kanadeva with a concrete example of the Wholeness of life, of Reality, and Kanadeva responded immediately by pointing to the other, complementary, aspect of our lives—the world of everyday life, of this and that, of utility and function. Everyday life penetrates Totality from top to bottom, with nothing spilling over, with nothing left out. Kanadeva thus followed Nagarjuna's lead perfectly.

In Zen lore, Nagarjuna is sometimes depicted as the full moon (of enlightenment)—or, as here, a full bowl. Furthermore, *Kanadeva* means "the one-eyed one," and in Zen literature much ado is made about the fact that a needle also has only one eye. In this literature, Kanadeva's one eye is often called the eye of nonduality.

Let's look at this story more closely. A needle is something useful; it has a purpose and a function. This is normal and appropriate. Yet the moment we step into the world of utility, function, and purpose—that is, the world of intention—we not only see multiplicity and duality, we can easily get taken in by them. We may quietly assume that the world is *only* multiplicity and duality.

But as human beings, we are capable of *seeing* more than this. We're capable of *seeing* that duality and Totality, delusion and enlightenment, samsara and Nirvana are not two.

As human beings, we suffer from the problem of self—that is, of seeing ourselves cut off and isolated in a world of other things. This leaves us full of wanting and craving and fearing and loathing. Nevertheless, we all have the capacity to *see* with the eye of nonduality, with an eye that can penetrate thoroughly and completely the Totality of life. We can experience the world as a Whole. This is what Kanadeva was expressing when he dropped the needle into the water.

When I draw a line like this:

---

from left to right ➞

and ask people what its opposite is, they usually draw a line like this:

⟵ *from right to left*

Yet if we look at the results, we can see that they're essentially the same.

This is indicative of our usual way of thinking and seeing. We see one thing, and we infer what we think of as its opposite.

But this ostensible opposite often appears much the same, if not identical.

For example, religious fanatics vigorously promote their viewpoints but are intolerant of the viewpoints of others. Meanwhile, other people scoff at them for being so narrow-minded. But if we look carefully at what the scoffers are thinking, it's virtually the same as the zealots: "You people are totally wrong. We know the right way to live and you don't." They mirror the people they criticize for their intolerance. This is the kind of thinking we often fall into once we see ourselves as separate, crystalline little things cut off from everything else.

What *is* opposite to a line drawn like this:

---

might be a line like this:

Rather than something straight and unchanging, we now have something that oscillates, that changes direction and moves about.

Here again, in another way, we find the water and the needle. We have something steady and straight; we also have its opposite, something that curves and changes. Woven together, the two demonstrate Reality.

Usually, when we find a dual pattern like this it immediately speaks to us, often on a very deep level. It occurs in many forms of music (chants, for example), in which we hear a steady drone and, superimposed on it, a melody. People generally take to this form of music quite naturally.

This pattern is indicative of something that we all truly *know*, deeply, within our hearts: there's an aspect of our lives that's steady and unchanging. It's not any particular thing; it's the Whole. It's utterly peaceful. Yet, at the same time, insepa-rable from it are all the ups and downs and ins and outs of life: things constantly changing, oscillating, coming, and going.

Our error is that much of the time we're entirely caught up only in the oscillating, the coming and going. We forget (or lose track of) the quiet, steady backdrop of Reality. We lose sight of the bowl. As a result, we fail to *see* what Nagarjuna points to. Indeed, we say it's cerebral, abstract, complex.

But that's not it at all. We've got it backward. It's not Real-ity but we ourselves who, lost in our concepts, are cerebral and abstract.

Keizan Jokin, the Zen teacher who compiled these stories of the ancient Zen ancestors, comments that if you drink Nagarjuna's water without understanding that there's a needle in it, the needle will get caught in your throat.

It's very easy for us to get caught by particulars, by specific details, by our own thoughts and emotions, by the world of utility and function. And when we do, we think we have to do something—to right ourselves, to fix the world, to straighten things out, to straighten other people out.

What we need to do instead is notice our own driven mind.

. . .

One more point to note regarding this first exchange between Nagarjuna and Kanadeva: their communication was not only immediate but wordless.

We live as though our lives—and enlightenment, and Reality itself—are things to view through a window or on a television screen. We live as though we're removed from our immediate situation. In other words, as the great Chinese Zen teacher Tung-shan would say, we live out our lives as though we are guest and not host.

But Truth is always with us. We only need to awaken to it. You can't seek it or find it, as though it were something removed from you or apart from you.

The life that is truly yours is inseparable from the life of the world itself. The gem is in your pocket now. It's been in your pocket all along. There's never been any need for you to acquire it.

Our business is to take care of *this moment*. It's always *this moment*.

In the end, it's you yourself who must live the practice and embrace the life you actually live. There's no one to check you at the door. You're free to walk in of your own accord right *now*. All you have to do is step through.

In realizing this, you begin to live your life with a different attitude, a different approach, a different understanding. Yet, outwardly, it looks very ordinary. You still eat food, breathe air, go to work. But inwardly there's a completely different awareness of what is taking place. Your life isn't contained in your goals or your memories or these few cubic feet of flesh. Your life is simply *this*, what is taking place *here, now*. There's no inside or outside to it.

Furthermore, you *see* that it's always been this way. It's the water and the needle; though they're not the same, they're not really two.

26

WHY SEEK

LIBERATION?

T HERE'S A STORY of a fellow who went to see a Zen teacher and asked, "I heard there was a buddha in ancient times who sat in meditation for ten eons but still did not achieve full liberation of mind. How could this be?"

The teacher said, "You've answered your own question."

"But he was meditating the whole time! Why didn't he wake up?"

The teacher replied, "He wasn't a buddha."

Like this fellow, we want explanations. We come to Zen, or to meditation, with some idea of what happens to people who practice hard. We think that people who are really serious about meditation must achieve something spectacular. We have all kinds of expectations—about what a buddha is, what enlightenment is, what liberation of mind is, what happens to you if you meditate a lot. And then we get upset when our expectations don't match up with Reality.

Yet most of us fail to see that it's our expectations that are the problem, not Reality.

We think that if we work very hard at something—say, becoming an astronomer or an auto mechanic—we can become good at it and perhaps master it. And sometimes that's true. The problem is that we come to meditation with this same kind of thinking. We even think of a Zen teacher as someone who has mastered the art of meditation.

If we approach Zen practice with that idea, however, then we don't understand it at all.

In this story, the questioner assumed that any hardworking and assiduous meditator would experience something special or come to some profound realization. After all, it seems only fair that if we work very hard at something for a long time, we should master it. Either that or we're likely to give it up.

In fact, people often *do* give up Zen practice after working very hard at it for some time. When it seems like they're not getting anywhere, they quit. But why didn't they get anywhere?

They—and we—don't get anywhere because we think we're doing something called "getting somewhere."

Zen practice isn't about getting somewhere. It isn't about becoming a buddha. In fact, that's impossible. Nothing *becomes* a buddha.

A buddha is simply a human being who is awake, aware of Reality. If you *see* how things are, what Reality is, then you're a buddha.

Still, we cling to the notion that "If I work very hard, maybe I can become enlightened—like a buddha." And then we begin practicing as if somehow we can acquire buddhahood.

But the fact of the matter is that you can't. You can't acquire it for a very simple reason: you are Buddha already. There's nothing for you to acquire.

Most of us approach Zen practice as if it offers something we need to get. But, actually, it's more like something to get rid of.

You already have everything you need to understand human life fully—not to be confused, not to be frightened, not to habitually long for things, not to suffer. All of this is already yours *right now*.

Yet we persist in thinking that we're lacking in some vital way, especially regarding enlightenment. And we get the idea that if we practice hard for a long time, then maybe we can become buddhas or become whole.

But Reality doesn't work that way. How can we gain something we already have, even if we practice meditation for eons? It's like yearning to be in America while you are living in New York.

We need to understand that the ancient meditator this fellow was asking about wasn't real. The questioner imagined him to be a person who was lacking and therefore had to meditate to become a buddha. But no such person actually exists—or ever does.

The fact is, no one who lives and walks among us lacks the ability to be awake, to be fully human, to realize the nature of Reality.

. . .

Here's another Zen story about a fellow who came to a Zen teacher seeking freedom of mind. The teacher asked him, "Who binds you?"

The man answered, "No one binds me."

"Then why seek liberation?"

We have a habit of going through life looking for something. We even read books like this one because we're trying to find something. But why seek something that's staring you in the face?

We spend our time caught up in thought, dividing everything off, separating ourselves from Reality—and then we think we lack something and have to fill that lack.

Unless we realize that this is what we do, we cannot become a buddha, simply because that kind of buddha is just an idea. And while you're caught up in that idea, you ignore or deny the clear and obvious Truth of *this very moment*.

Buddhas are those who are aware of their own delusions. We may think they have some special insight, but, actually, they merely *see* how we play this game. They *see* how we're duped into it. And they *see* how painful it is to play the game without realizing what we're doing.

Zen practice is about acquainting ourselves on a daily basis with how quickly we're tricked, how easily we're sucked into our own ideas of reality, and how tightly we're bound up in our petty likes and dislikes, our fears and prejudices.

Nevertheless, we're *here*. We can't help but be *here*. In Reality, you are Buddha. Already. *This* is going on. We only miss it because we always make something of it. We make something of what is nothing in particular.

Zen teaching and meditation are not about finding or attaining anything. They're about noticing what our actual situation is. And your actual situation is that you're not lacking a thing.

All you have to do is just realize what is going on. *This* is what meditation is about—the practice of Awareness. *Thus.*

The world isn't any way in particular—but, moment after moment, it's always vibrant, unpredictable, and Real. All we need to do is *see* how it is, that it's *just this*—immediately at hand.

PART TWO

PURE MIND

27

PURE MIND

M IND IS BASIC. Mind is primary. Mind is ever-present in each situation. For anything to be happening in *this moment*, Mind is necessarily present. Mind is the basis for *this*, for what's going on *now*.

This is the very heart of what the Buddha taught: "Everything is founded on Mind, is made of Mind. To act or speak with a pure mind is happiness."

But is it really possible for us to speak or act from such a mind? And just what is a pure mind, anyway?

A pure mind enters freely into each situation, no matter what it is. We may feel sadness, remorse, or grief, but if our mind is pure, it all sweeps through. It doesn't take hold anywhere; it doesn't grind us up. There's nothing in the mind to obstruct the emotion, so it doesn't get caught. We feel no need to avoid it, block it, take hold of it, work it up into something bigger, or make something else out of it.

There's a story of a Zen teacher who cried when his wife died. His students were very surprised by this. "You're enlightened! Why are you crying?"

The teacher simply said matter-of-factly, "I'll miss her."

What his students were really saying was, "We didn't think you were human!"

It's nonsense, of course. A Zen teacher is a human being, with human emotions. Yet many people have this erroneous impression that once we wake up we won't (or shouldn't) have deep or powerful emotions anymore. Such an impression is pure delusion. Why would awakening cause us to suddenly relinquish all human feeling, to become something other than human?

With a pure mind, our feelings are not fundamentally different. But what we do with them (or, more appropriately, stop doing with them) is very different indeed.

The Buddha also said, "Everything is founded on Mind, is made of Mind. To act or speak with a corrupt mind is misery." What does it mean to act or speak with a corrupt mind?

A corrupt mind is a fractured, splintered, broken, divided mind—a mind that sees this as opposed to that. It's the mind of self and other, of separation and alienation—in other words, our ordinary mind.

In a corrupt mind, emotions and ideas arise, just as they do in a pure mind—but then we grab hold of them rather than let them pass through and sweep away. We hold them close and build all kinds of mental structures around them. We carry them around with us, identify with them, and put them on display.

In other words, a corrupt mind is removed from the Whole. It's the mind of ego, a mind that views everything as though apart from itself. It's a mind that gets caught up in greediness, selfishness, fear, longing, loathing, and grasping.

The Buddha did not hesitate to call this mind "misery."

Zen practice is about recognizing this corrupt mind for what it is. It's about *seeing* what's going on in each moment without grasping it, without blocking it. It's *seeing* the folly and misery of the corrupt mind, *seeing* that trying to take control only creates pain. This *seeing* is itself an expression of a pure mind.

We're always dealing with *now*, with what is actually taking place. Thus, in Zen practice, our focus is on what's going on in our mind *now*.

Misery of any kind—whether it's fear, anger, loneliness, sadness, or grief—has grasping in it. To the extent that we learn to recognize this, we can let it go, let it wash through.

This is the practice of meditation. As we sit in meditation, thoughts keep coming up. Sometimes they can be disturbing. Sometimes they're wonderful. But they keep coming. And sometimes we grab on to them. We build upon them, constructing whole mental worlds. This is the corrupt mind Buddha spoke of.

Our practice is to *see* that we do this.

Another common error of a corrupt mind is thinking that we have to let go—as if letting go is a specific, willful act. But it's not, just as falling asleep naturally is not.

In our ignorance, we try deliberately, forcibly to let go of our thoughts. We try to control a process of letting go. But this will never work. Just as you can't force yourself to go to sleep, you can't force yourself to wake up.

You only need to *see* to let go. Indeed, to *just see* is to let go—or, rather, it's not to take hold of anything in the first place.

Mind is already *here;* thus a pure mind is always possible for us. We only have to be scrupulously honest with ourselves.

Purity and freedom are immediate. We only need to *see,* let them sweep through, and not interfere.

28

THE THING WELL MADE

T HE HALCYON DAYS are two weeks of calm weather sur-
rounding the winter solstice. They are a time to reflect—a dark and brooding time when we may be drawn into
quiet contemplation on the past year as well as on larger dimensions and aspects of our lives.

In his poem "Halcyon Days," Walt Whitman conjures up
the rich imagery that this season inspires, but Whitman uses
the term metaphorically to refer to the happiness and tranquillity found in the waning days of a long life well lived.

Whitman's poem is from a section of *Leaves of Grass* entitled "Sands at Seventy." It's an elderly Walt Whitman writing,
but this poem speaks to all ages of life. As Whitman notes,
youth is a wonderful time of life. But so is middle age. And so
is childhood. And so, too, is old age. It's all wonderful and
good, and in just a few lines Whitman brings this out with his
inimitable gusto:

Not from successful love alone,
Nor wealth, nor honor'd middle age, nor victories of
*   politics or war;*
But as life wanes, and all the turbulent passions calm,
As gorgeous, vapory, silent hues cover the evening sky,
As softness, fulness, rest, suffuse the frame, like fresher,
*   balmier air,*
As the days take on a mellower light, and the apple at last
*   hangs really finish'd and indolent-ripe on the tree,*
Then for the teeming quietest, happiest days of all!
The brooding and blissful halcyon days!

Fulfillment does not come from successful love or wealth or middle age or victories, yet Whitman pays tribute to those times in our lives when we are active with much planning for the future, with the accumulation of goods, and with the gains of power and reputation. For Whitman these are all delicious burdens.

Yet Whitman reminds us not to forget that as life wanes, here we also find something rich and beautiful. If we look only to earlier, more exciting and dynamic aspects of our life, or if we think that growing into old age is dreadful, then we've missed out on something truly precious.

In our youth we're preoccupied with sorting out everything and making arrangements for ourselves—in schooling, career, marriage, child rearing. What are we going to become? What are we to do with our lives? What are our interests? Our talents? What's important to us? How shall we guide ourselves? It's a turbulent time of questions, duties, obligations, and responsibilities. But as life wanes, this has all been settled for good or ill, and now life takes on a mellower glow. We settle into a quieter time, when we are "really finished," like an apple that hangs, fully ripened, on the tree.

The French have a phrase, *la chose bien faite*—the thing well made, the thing well done, or the life well lived. Zen practice goes to the heart of this same matter—doing and living well, doing and living fully, doing and living our best.

Throughout most of our lives, we're so caught up in this and that, rushing through these wonderful distractions and stages, that we don't (or can't) take the time to settle into the mellow light that's always there and to let freshness suffuse the frame. Thus we miss this simple matter of just doing and living fully.

Actor Peter O'Toole once told of receiving a coat he had sent to the cleaners. It came back with a note pinned to the inside that read, "It distresses us to return work that is not perfect."

This, to me, is what it means to be fully human. Not that we must be perfect or that we *can* bring everything to perfection or completion but, rather, that it is our concern that we do so.

This is precisely what Zen practice is about: doing our best. Whatever we're doing—whether it be humble or grand—we take care of it all in each moment, from beginning to end. Thus we arrive at completion in each moment.

Zen is not about arriving at some end point in the future. In fact, there *is* no such thing. We have no guarantee of an old age. Rather, in each moment, we live life completely, whole-heartedly, totally. We attend fully to *this moment* and to what is brought forth in it, yet we are not attached to the result.

When I was about twenty, I developed a passion for the music of Gustav Mahler. I decided to make a collage formed of repeated images of the composer to hang on my wall. I designed it from a high-contrast photograph I had of Mahler from one of my albums. But I needed more copies of the image. Since it was in stark black and white, I thought it would be easy to duplicate.

This was before there were any copy shops or photocopiers around. If you wanted to run off prints of anything, you had to go to a print shop. I asked the man at the nearby print shop if he could reproduce the photo. He wasn't sure, since there were a few subtle grays in the picture, but he said he'd give it a try. He asked me to come back in a couple of hours.

I returned with my brother awhile later, but the man at the print shop wasn't done with the photo. He showed me what he had produced. I thought it looked fine, but he said he wasn't satisfied. He wouldn't let it go. He returned to his shop to work on it some more, leaving my brother and me to wait out front.

Young and impatient, I started to become annoyed. But my brother, who is twelve years older than me and was an artist and a teacher, was very sensitive to such things. As I began to fume and complain, he said calmly, "The man is a craftsman."

His words almost knocked me over. Suddenly I realized that this man was engaged in his work in a way that I had never considered before. He wasn't just going to hand over any old thing. This was his life. And the quality of his life was manifested in what he created. It distressed him to return work that wasn't his best.

Even though I couldn't see what was wrong with the images he showed me, and even though I was willing to pay for them as they were, he refused to consider his job done. He was indeed a true craftsman.

Eventually he did get them good enough to part with them, but this incident, small as it seemed, made an enormous impression on me. It told me a great deal about how one should conduct one's life.

Not long after this I began to develop an interest in Buddhism and Zen. Though I didn't appreciate it at the time, the incident at the print shop did a lot to prepare my mind to hear what my Zen teacher had to say.

There were other influences, too. I had an uncle who was a carpenter. He was already a very old man when I was a child. He had been a carpenter all his life, but after he retired he went blind. Still, he would make things—even complicated pieces with fitted joints. Everyone was amazed at what he could do. But he had been working with wood and saws and chisels his whole life. His knowledge and skill were all in his bones, his mind, his heart, and his hands.

I remember one time I came upon him working in his shop. I watched him from the basement stairs. I don't know if he was even aware that I was there. He just kept working at a slow, steady pace.

What most impressed me was how he would pick up a piece of wood. I never saw anyone handle an object like that before. It was all in his hands. He would caress the wood. I could tell that he knew a great deal about what he was touching because there seemed to be no gap between his hands and the wood or between his hands and his tools.

Yet my uncle didn't need to exert himself. His exercise, his practice, his learning were done. He knew in one touch what a younger, less experienced person would need years to learn.

To live life fully, we need to burn it completely through in each moment. This is merging with our object, with whatever we're taking up.

Eventually, whatever we truly take up becomes a part of our life. We've digested it. We know it beyond merely having an idea of it. It's in our hands and fingers, our bones and marrow. And now we no longer find it necessary to strain ourselves.

As Whitman points out, a life that is full and complete in this way embraces all—the sad, the sorrowful, the exciting, the wonderful, the years of anticipation, the years of power and gain, and the time of facility and know-how. It's all *here* and *now*, being expressed as one's life.

My uncle was not a young man when I knew him. He couldn't get out and play baseball as he once had. His life was quieter. But it was still teeming, still full of energy—but of a different sort.

After ripening into old age, having experienced much of life, we can now think quietly, dispassionately, on what we've learned. Thus even old age can be a time of new hatchings and of new things to come.

When we learn to live life completely, wholly, and fully in each moment, we can live content with what we bring to each event, without depending on someone or something else to complete us from the outside. In this full realization of our lives, there *is* no "outside," for in a life really finished, the bonds of self have been released.

29

TRANSFORMING
HEART AND MIND

Z EN IS ABOUT the total transformation of heart and mind. If you realize Zen, it transforms you totally, completely.

Of course, you're always being totally transformed in every moment, whether or not you encounter Zen. But if you don't attend to just how you're being transformed, you're not likely to wake up.

It's commonly thought that to live a full life we must set goals for ourselves. And if we've taken up Zen, we might think our goal is to reach enlightenment. But Zen is not about devising a target that we have to hit and then putting a lot of time and energy into hitting it. This is just our ordinary way of thinking—our habitual, locked-in approach to life and to the world. It's just more entanglement and confusion.

Zen is freedom from all entanglements. It's coming into this moment and *seeing* what's going on, before we make up all kinds of hypotheses and explanations.

There's a Taoist story that illustrates this point. It's about a man, Chi Ch'ang, who wanted to become the greatest archer in the world. He set out to find the greatest teacher of archery, who he had heard was a fellow named Wei Fei.

The first thing Wei Fei told Chi Ch'ang was that he had to learn not to blink. So Chi Ch'ang would lie beneath his wife's loom with his eyes wide open, letting the lint and dust from the loom settle in them. He finally realized that he had mastered not blinking when a spider wove a web through his eyelashes.

He went to Wei Fei and, with pride, demonstrated his accomplishment. Wei Fei told him flatly that now he had to learn to see. He showed Chi Ch'ang how to look at things until, after long practice, Chi Ch'ang could see the details on a willow leaf at a hundred paces.

Now, Wei Fei said, Chi Ch'ang was ready to learn how to shoot.

Chi Ch'ang studied with Wei Fei for many years and eventually mastered how to shoot. He then went about showing off his feats of skill. He would balance glasses of water on his elbow while shooting a hundred arrows into a willow leaf at a hundred paces without spilling a drop.

But Chi Ch'ang hadn't yet achieved his goal of being the greatest archer in the world. There was still one thing standing in his way: Wei Fei, his teacher. While Chi Ch'ang had attained a level of competence as great as his teacher's, as long as Wei Fei lived, he would never surpass him.

One day, as Wei Fei stepped into a clearing, Chi Ch'ang, who had been lying in wait, let fly an arrow straight to Wei Fei's heart. Wei Fei, however, being very discerning, realized what was happening, took an arrow from his quiver, and shot Chi Ch'ang's arrow right out of the air. A strange battle then ensued. With each arrow Chi Ch'ang let fly, Wei Fei countered it with another. Arrows met in midair, one after another, until finally Wei Fei had no arrows left. Chi Ch'ang shot his last arrow, and as it streaked toward Wei Fei's heart, Wei Fei plucked off a nearby twig. At the last instant, he used it to deflect Chi Ch'ang's arrow to the ground at his feet.

At this point, both men were so overwhelmed by their magnificent show of skill that they ran up and embraced each other. Wei Fei, however, realized the danger he was in. He told Chi Ch'ang that there was an even greater archer, Kan Ying, who made the two of them look like fumbling little children.

Chi Ch'ang's pride was injured by having his accomplishments described as child's play. He immediately set out to find Kan Ying. His quest took him into strange and distant lands.

Eventually, in a cave on a high mountain, Chi Ch'ang found Kan Ying. He was very old, far older than anyone Chi Ch'ang had ever seen. "I've come to see if I am indeed as great an archer as I think I am," Chi Ch'ang bellowed. He took his bow, notched an arrow, and shot down a goose flying high overhead. The old man, seeming unimpressed, leaped out onto a narrow ledge suspended thousands of feet above a gorge and called to

Chi Ch'ang to come to him. Chi Ch'ang, too proud to decline, jumped onto the ledge. But immediately he grew dizzy and his mind began to spin. He could only kneel down and crawl back off the ledge.

As Chi Ch'ang tried to regain his composure, he looked back to see Kan Ying pointing to a bird flying so high above that it looked no bigger than a sesame seed. He also noticed that Kan Ying had no bow. Nevertheless, he notched an invisible arrow and, with a swishing sound, let it fly. The unseen arrow hit its mark and took down the bird.

Chi Ch'ang realized he still had much to learn.

The story does not say just what he learned, but after ten years with Kan Ying, Chi Ch'ang returned to his village. Everyone remembered him for his arrogance and conceit, but now they could see that he had completely transformed. Gone was his look of disdain and self-importance. Gone, too, was his bow. Still, it was obvious that he had learned something profound, and the villagers all waited for the great feats of bowmanship he would no doubt soon display.

But Chi Ch'ang never showed them. As time passed and he grew older, he demonstrated nothing. Nevertheless, stories of his great skill spread far and wide.

Just before he died, while visiting a friend, he noticed a bow in a corner. "That instrument in the corner," asked Chi Ch'ang, "what do you call it, and for what purpose is it used?" His friend said, "Oh, master! Now I see that you are indeed the greatest archer in all the land, for only then could you have forgotten the bow, both its name and its use."

Shortly after that Chi Ch'ang died. It was said that in his village, for a time, artists threw away their brushes and carpenters were ashamed to be seen with their rules.

It's not an oversight that the story doesn't tell us what brought about Chi Ch'ang's total transformation. The fact is that no one can say.

It's critical that we understand this. There's nothing specific that we can point to that went into Chi Ch'ang's transformation of heart and mind.

What Chi Ch'ang acquired through *seeing* and understanding is that there's nothing "out there" to get, to master, to seize, to acquire. He realized that Reality is forever right *here*, that what is to be mastered is the life we're living *right now*, *right here*, from moment to moment. Chi Ch'ang learned to be free of a longing heart—to be free of the desire to make himself into something special.

At some point we have to realize, as Chi Ch'ang did, what this practice is about. It's about freedom of mind, about not getting caught in goals or pride or ideas. It's not about abandoning our lives. It's not even about abandoning our goals. But it is about nonattachment, about being able to move through this world in a completely ordinary way, yet freely, without being taken in by the things we see and touch and hear.

As long as we maintain the mind that Chi Ch'ang manifested early in his life, we really don't understand anything about

Zen teaching or practice. We're just caught up in our ordinary, greedy, grasping way of life.

We must remind ourselves of the actual circumstances we're in and notice this grasping mind that holds one thing apart from and above another. We need to recognize that the source of our confusion and pain is this very leaning of mind itself.

By acquainting ourselves with our own heart and mind— *seeing* their fearful, grasping, and greedy nature—we are transformed. This is how we are freed of confusion and pain.

30

TRUTH IS NOTHING
IN PARTICULAR

AFTER KATAGIRI ROSHI gave me permission to do a little teaching, it took me only a short time to realize how impossible it was to teach anything about Truth. I'd try to make a point, but every time I'd say something I felt I had to tack on, "Well, that's not quite what I meant." I soon realized that I could never actually say what I meant. Not fully. What I was trying to do was literally impossible.

I wanted to quit. I went to Katagiri Roshi and told him of my misgivings. "We can't talk about this," I said.

"But you have to say something," he replied. "If you don't say anything, nobody will understand."

Usually when people tell you something, they literally mean what they say. But Dharma words are never offered in this way. Nothing is being presented that you are expected to take, memorize, or add to your idea bank. You already have whatever the Dharma teaching is pointing out. Dharma words are more like a reminder to take note of what you already *see* and *know* but have long forgotten.

We sometimes find it disquieting just to sit and listen, not taking hold of anything. We hear a Dharma talk, and afterward when someone asks us about it, we say, "It was good."

"What was it about?" they ask.

To our surprise, we find we can't say. Still, we feel like we got a lot out of the talk, even though we didn't walk away with anything particular—that is, with anything we could grasp.

It's a subtle point, but we need to come back and hear it repeatedly: Dharma teachings are unlike all other kinds of teaching. Dharma teaching never says, "Here it is; this is what you need to know; this is what you should believe." Instead, Dharma teaching is about waking up to what cannot be put into words, what cannot be grasped, what cannot be conceptualized—but what can only be pointed out, can only be directly *seen.*

Two Zen students are talking. The first one says, "Zen is hard practice. You have to discipline yourself, day and night." The other responds, "That's not true at all. Zen is natural and easy, just like flowing water seeking its level."

The first student is convinced she's right, so she decides to go to the teacher for confirmation. "Zen practice is difficult," she begins. "It takes a lot of hard work and discipline. Isn't that so?"

The teacher looks at her and says, "You're right."

Delighted that the teacher has confirmed her understanding, she immediately seeks out the other student and confronts him. "Roshi agrees with me!" she says. "Zen practice is hard work."

The second student thinks, "How can this be? Zen is natural. There's nothing difficult about it at all." And so off he goes to see the teacher.

"Zen is natural and easy," he begins. "It's like leaves tumbling from the trees in autumn. Wouldn't you agree?"

"You're right," the teacher tells him.

Unfortunately, the teacher's attendant has been on hand to hear both of these encounters. After the second student leaves, he can no longer contain himself. "Wait a minute!" he blurts out. "You told the first one that she was right when she said that Zen is difficult, and you told the second that he was right when he said that Zen is easy. Well, which is it? It can't be both!"

"You're right," says the teacher.

What are we to make of such a story? Is it just silly? Stupid? Contradictory? Irrational? (If you think that the Zen teacher will just keep saying "you're right" to anything people ask, you're wrong.)

The problem we fall into is that we try to take hold of things. And as long as we do, we'll not *see* what this story is pointing to—that the Real World, which is always in full view, is always just beyond our conceptual grasp. Though Reality can be pointed to, it can't be directly spoken of or described.

It's so much easier for us to grasp at explanations and stories than to *just see.* As we box up the world in our minds, we keep insisting that things must be like this or they must be like that—or else we decide that the whole thing is ridiculous. Or, if we feel magnanimous, we might say something like, "Yes, for you it's like that, but for me it's like this." In doing any of these things, we miss (or avoid or ignore) Reality.

We need to stop looking for a particular thing, a particular concept, a particular teaching, a particular answer to bail us out. We fail to *see* that whatever we would take hold of is cut and removed from the Whole. We simply will not find Truth—Dharma, Reality—within our ideas and beliefs.

We live through experience, not through description. Though we want to share our experiences with others, we actually can't. To share a sunset with someone, there's no point in describing the sunset (or debating about how best to describe it). Just stand next to the person and watch the sun go down without saying a word.

The ultimate failing of a teacher is to believe that what they tell their students is Truth. When the student takes hold of that belief, such a teacher will be incapable of taking it away and thus letting the student taste freedom.

Ultimately, we need to abandon any notion that taking hold of some particular thing—some particular idea, belief, ritual, religion, perspective, form of dress, or way of acting—is going to bring us to Truth. Finally we have to stop looking for something to save us, something to stand under, to identify with, to improve us, to make us whole.

We must abandon understanding and being understood. As we do, we can come into *this moment,* fully alive and awake.

31

WITHOUT RELIGIOUS
EGOTISM

ZEN PRACTICE is cultivating a mind that doesn't act out of difference alone—that is, out of the part or the self. It is cultivating a mind that comes out of the Whole—that *sees* the Whole picture in which we're all acting, in which we all take part, and which sustains all. Cultivating such a mind is sometimes called the practice of egolessness.

But this doesn't happen to us automatically simply because we meditate or listen to lectures on Buddhism or read Buddhist books or call ourselves Buddhists. Real effort, properly directed, is required. And this effort is not about going "out there" and straightening out this fluid, inconceivable world; rather, it's primarily about learning to *look* deeply into our own lives and hearts and realizing where our difficulties and confusion come from.

Buddhist teachings and practice all have to do with this issue—this basic confusion, this problem we have with self.
Thus Zen is a very no-nonsense practice.

We can't just go through the motions of Zen practice—
sitting in meditation, reading books, attending classes, going
to workshops and retreats—as if studying the Buddhadharma
were just another self-help program. This practice is not about
helping the self. It's about *seeing* this so-called self for what it
is—an illusion.

This means that we have to actually deal with stuff, mull
things over, look at what's going on, and work at it. In short,
we have to actually *see* what we're doing.

Our problem is not out there in the world. It's not a matter
of straightening "them" out or fixing a particular situation.
It's a matter of observing our own cast of mind.

There's a story of a Zen teacher who particularly praised one
of his students. Several people were bewildered by this and
wanted to know what was so special about him.

"Come with me," the teacher said and led them to where
the student was living. The teacher knocked on the door. From
within they heard a pen being tossed down, papers being
shuffled, a book being closed, and then footsteps. The door
opened and a young man said, "Yes?"

"Sorry, wrong room," said the teacher.

They proceeded to the next room, where the teacher again
knocked. Immediately they heard footsteps. The door opened
and a young man said, "Yes?"

"May we come in?" asked the teacher. The student obliged.

Inside the room, on a table, was a sheet of paper with a drawn circle, begun but abandoned halfway. The student was still holding a calligraphy brush in his hand. He had obviously started drawing a circle but had been interrupted midway by the knock at the door.

The teacher then turned to his guests and said, "You can teach someone like this."

This teacher knew that it's much easier to teach someone who is willing to drop his own plan, her own agenda. This was why the teacher found the student so refreshing. Such a person can quickly learn from a true teacher, if they are fortunate enough to find one.

Much of Zen may at first seem baffling or contradictory to us. But over time, with effort and attention, these seeming contradictions will begin to clear up.

I certainly ran into this repeatedly with my own teacher. He often said things that at first struck me as bizarre, ridiculous, or just plain wrong. But I gave him the benefit of the doubt, though I kept my eyes open, and gradually I learned what he had to show me. After a while, I started to see that many of the apparent ambiguities, contradictions, paradoxes, and enigmas of Zen weren't really contradictory or ambiguous. They only seemed that way because of the presumptions and unexamined leanings of my own mind.

It wasn't easy for me, after meeting Katagiri Roshi. I almost quit Zen three times—twice because I got to thinking that Zen was nuts, once after I'd been with him awhile because I thought I wasn't up to it. But I didn't quit. And while there may have been a few things about my training that were less than ideal (how could there not be?), he pointed out everything I needed to see. Still, whether I learned anything from him or not was up to me. He didn't interfere. He was a very good teacher.

And I would never have learned from him had I not willingly set aside my own notions and predilections at a few critical junctures. With his guidance, I was able to hold my opinions and beliefs loosely in one hand while turning over and freely examining what he was showing me with the other.

It's essential that we loosen our grip on our cherished ideas, attitudes, and approaches, in the same way that the calligrapher student left off with drawing his circle. If you hold tight to some particular notion—about the world, about what's fair, about Buddhism, about who you are—there will be interference and resistance to what a teacher points out, and you'll not really *see*. Or else you'll just get another idea, which you'll exchange for some idea you believed before. If you do this, you're just eating Zen candy. There's no transformation of heart and mind, and the background confusion remains unaltered.

At the same time, however, we need to realize that the opposite approach—swallowing whole whatever a teacher gives you without examining it critically, openly, carefully, fairly, and respectfully—will prove just as barren. Blind, mindless acceptance isn't openness; it's simply another form of grasping—in this case, clinging to the notion that whatever your teacher tells you must be true.

We need to take to heart these words of the Buddha:

Don't believe me because you see me as your teacher. Don't believe me because others do. And don't believe anything because you've read it in a book, either. Don't put your faith in reports or tradition or hearsay or the authority of religious leaders or texts. Don't rely on mere logic or inference or appearances or speculation. Know for yourselves that certain things are unwholesome and wrong. And when you do, then give them up. And when you know for yourselves that certain things are wholesome and good, then accept them and follow them.

Another way of looking at this is through the Buddha's teaching of avoiding of extremes. Don't be a hundred percent gullible; don't be a hundred percent scornful and dismissive, either. The Buddhadharma urges each of us to be good skeptics—in the classical Greek sense. A good skeptic is slightly gullible: willing to consider and examine any evidence or argument being raised, at least temporarily. They neither swallow it whole nor reject it outright. They continuously observe it, test it, and engage it with interest, curiosity, and openness.

To dismiss something as bunk before you examine it is the hallmark of a believer, not a skeptic. Those who won't even examine something are operating out of an agenda, are shut down to actual experience, and are so full of ideas that they can't see what's coming at them. For them the world is structured and fixed, and they're often caught up in their own form of bunk: an insistence on dismissing and devaluing certain propositions or attitudes. This is not skepticism but cynicism.

In order to cultivate a pure mind, we need to set aside our personal agendas. But this doesn't mean taking up the personal agenda of someone else—a teacher, for example. No true Dharma teachers would ever direct you to follow their personal agenda. In fact, they really don't have much of a personal agenda regarding you. Their only concern for you is that you awaken. (As my teacher used to say, the final job of a teacher is to free the student of the teacher.)

Many of us initially take up the religious life with a lot of high-minded ideas about what we're going to accomplish. But that's only more ego, more business as usual—religious egotism. If we truly want to live the religious life, we simply have to drop our agendas—even our religious ones. Only then can we begin to cultivate a mind of true goodness and compassion, which comes out of a concern for the Whole.

As we live out of such a mind, we become generous, with no sense of giving or of making a sacrifice. We become open, with no sense of tolerance. We become patient, with no sense of putting up with anything. We become compassionate, with no sense of separation. And we become wise, with no sense of having to straighten anyone out.

32

GETTING OUT OF
YOUR MIND

MOST PEOPLE START OUT practicing Zen with an ordinary mind—that is, with the idea that they're going
to benefit from it somehow, that it will make them healthier or
happier or more grounded or more spiritual or that it will improve them in some other way.

Indeed, most of us generally approach everything with the
idea that we're going to get something from it. After all, if we
don't or won't or can't, why should we bother?

This is ordinary Zen, not actual Zen.

Ordinary Zen can take many forms, depending on what we
expect to get out of it. The most common is simply practicing
for yourself. *You* want enlightenment. *You* want to end your
personal pain and suffering. *You* want to be a Zen hotshot.
This is where most of us start.

Eventually, however, we might get wind of the free-floating notion that we're supposed to take up Zen for the benefit of all beings. This usually means that we're learning to direct our minds toward others. But without a deep understanding of the inter-identity of self and other, we're likely to create a facade of altruism that merely masks our continuing concern for self as our motive. *We* want to help all beings. *We* want to be one with others. *We* want to have less selfish motives. This, too, falls short of actual Zen.

Or we may practice in the expectation of having a mystical experience—communing with God, perhaps, or dissolving in a flood of bliss or energy. This is fine, but it's not really Zen. In fact, this kind of approach and understanding is not even Buddhist.

In Zen there's no ulterior motive. In Zen we practice for the sake of practice.

What's critical is motive. If you take up Zen for some other purpose, it's not Zen, even though it may look like Zen. Instead, it's confusion—just business as usual.

We often want to involve ourselves with things that are special, wonderful, and powerful. From the outside, Zen can certainly look like it's all of these—or perhaps like it will imbue us with these qualities. Such thoughts are pure delusion. Zen is none of the above.

Zen teacher Bankei was a popular lecturer who could draw large crowds. One day a student from another Buddhist sect, jealous of Bankei's large audience, interrupted one of his talks in an effort to draw him into a debate.

"The founder of my sect," said the student, "could stand on one side of the river while his attendant, standing on the opposite bank, would hold up a blank sheet of paper. With brush in hand, our founder could write the name of Buddha through the air. What about you?"

"That's a good trick," said Bankei, "but it's not the way of Zen. My miracle is to *just eat* when hungry and to *just drink* when thirsty."

We really need to get this straight. Zen is not about something miraculous or about cultivating special powers of any kind. It's found in the everyday, in the unexceptional.

Here's the irony: when we enter into Zen practice thinking we are cultivating something special, we remain locked in ordinary mind, in our ordinary ways of thinking about gain and goals and results.

Simone Weil wrote, "Our mediocre self is not afraid to experience fatigue and pain. It is afraid of being killed."

Look at how much pain and suffering so many of us endure in our lives—to get the degree, to get the job, to impress others, to impress ourselves, to please others, or to make ourselves happy. We drive ourselves to get this, to accomplish that. And in the process, we put up with—and we create—enormous pain and suffering.

But in Zen this is not the point. We somehow think we have to endure pain and suffering and through this we'll find our way to enlightenment.

It doesn't work that way. Though we might endure pain and suffering, if we haven't looked at our motive, we're still confused, still unhappy.

What are we actually afraid of? We're not afraid of putting up with pain, suffering, fatigue, or of driving ourselves. In fact, we're afraid of being killed. We're afraid of egolessness.

Most of us keep ourselves from being killed in all sorts of clever and desperate ways—by building a reputation, by acquiring power or wealth, by creating grand goals for ourselves, by trying to conform or not to conform. This approach typically results in some form of "look at me" Zen. We get into Zen big time. We do a lot of meditation retreats. We acquire robes. We pare down our lifestyle. The irony is that none of this is Zen. It's all just more delusion.

Most of us are actually afraid of freedom. We say, in effect, "I don't want this thing called freedom because I'm afraid people won't notice me. I'll be forgotten, marginalized, left behind. I'm afraid I'll fade into oblivion." And so we drive ourselves mercilessly (and sometimes drive ourselves mad) in those areas where we're not afraid—enduring fatigue, suffering, and pain.

Zen practice ("right effort," as taught by the Buddha) is not about straining, striving, and struggling. Rather, it's about taking up the activity of the moment. In listening, it's to *just listen;* in doing the dishes, it's to *just do the dishes;* in driving, it's to *just drive.* It's to drink when you're thirsty, to eat when you're hungry.

We think we want enlightenment, and that's our very problem. We want to get it—and we want to know when we've got it—so we can possess it and enjoy it. Instead of running the movie called delusion that we're always looking at, we want to view the movie called enlightenment. Yet in holding our delusion at arm's length, we hold enlightenment at arm's length as well.

Here's yet more irony: if we would just notice that we're doing this, we'd be enlightened on the spot. We step into enlightenment when we simply learn not to deceive ourselves.

We look to the ancient Zen masters, thinking they must have had special powers and abilities we'd like to cultivate in ourselves. Yet we don't realize what we're doing. We're only thinking of ourselves. And then we wonder why we don't awaken.

It's because this practice is so simple that it's easy to slip off, to be distracted, to miss the point.

My own teacher used to say that Zen practice often seems difficult and complicated, but it's not. It's our minds and thoughts that are complicated, and so we complicate our lives.

Zen practice is about *seeing* how we do this. And how, when we do, what comes of it—pain, fatigue, and suffering. Little by little, however, without struggling and striving but simply through *seeing*, we learn to step away from such entanglements.

It all boils down to motive. Is it about getting something or achieving something—or is it simply to be awake?

33

FORSAKING

UNDERSTANDING

B UDDHIST LITERATURE often uses the term *bodhisattva*, which literally means "an enlightenment being"—a wise and compassionate person of high moral caliber who vows to save all beings from suffering and distress. This may sound special, but in fact a bodhisattva comes into the world in very much the same way a pedestrian does.

Right now, you're probably not a pedestrian. But the moment you set this book down and go for a walk, you're a pedestrian—you're traveling on foot. Suddenly, a pedestrian has come into the world. Yet from moment to moment, there's no particular person who is inherently and consistently a pedestrian. The moment you stop walking, the pedestrian suddenly disappears.

In much the same way bodhisattvas come into the world. In any given moment, a bodhisattva can suddenly appear. In one moment it may be you. In the next, it may be someone else.

If we think the term *bodhisattva* refers to a particular person born at a particular time who somehow has had special powers since birth (or is destined to develop them), then we've misunderstood the down-to-earth, practical nature of a bodhisattva. Just as in any moment you can become a pedestrian, at any time, without calculation or planning, you can become a bodhisattva.

I'm not speaking of anything ephemeral, distant, or supernatural. This is the Reality of our lives. It all unfolds in just this way. Nothing is inherently anything in particular. It's all very dynamic, very practical, very earthy.

It is said that a bodhisattva comes into the world forsaking both understanding and being understood. This is true.

When I went through lay ordination with my teacher, he stamped a Chinese character on the back of my *rakusu* (a miniature Zen robe, which looks a little like a bib, worn around the neck). The character means "no understanding" and is also translated as "not knowing" or "no knowing." At the time I was profoundly disappointed to hear this. I thought Zen was about understanding—of coming to some realization about the world and our situation in it. I was very confused by this. But this "no understanding" is central to Buddhist practice and to realization.

In fact, the Buddha said there are two kinds of knowledge. The first he called "knowing accordingly"—knowing what things look like, sound like, and appear to be. This kind of knowledge involves ideas, concepts, and the surface appearance of seemingly separate things. Knowing accordingly takes place in the realm of objects, of separation, of this and that, of our typical fractured view of the world.

Most of the time we act as though this kind of knowing can lead to (or at least reflect) Reality and Truth. But the moment we dig beneath the surface a little, we're left with *not* knowing. This scares, worries, and unnerves us.

Often, in response, we make the mistake of thinking that somehow, if we can get the right kind of surface knowledge—the *right* ideas—then we'll get to the bottom of things.

But undulating, dynamic, ever-changing Reality cannot be understood by means of knowing accordingly. It's simply the wrong tool for the job. It's like trying to draw water with a sieve; even the best, most painstakingly crafted sieve won't suffice.

Nevertheless, it's quite possible to *know* Reality. Indeed, Reality is all we can and do *know*.

Yet there's nothing we can say about Reality, really, because there's only constant flux and change. The moment we say something, we immediately freeze a tiny piece of it, a tiny instant. But since Reality is never actually frozen, whatever we say can never hit upon (or lead us to) Truth. Truth simply won't go into words.

Still, we can *see* it.

Thus the Buddha also spoke of a second kind of Knowledge—of awakening to Truth, of *seeing* that we can't pin down Reality, that the world is fluid rather than frozen. This is *seeing*

Reality not just on the surface but through and through. The Buddha called this *seeing* "penetration."

We're always dealing with *right here, right now*—and with what is showing up *right here, right now*. And in learning to be *right here, right now,* we can come to *see* that any given thing, if we don't freeze it too solid in our minds, is utterly fluid and capable of expressing itself in any number of ways.

The fact is, we can't adequately say or explain or get an idea of how anything is. Penetration is *seeing* this directly. It's a quiet but profound understanding of *this moment* that is not bound up in ideas of "me" or "I have this understanding."

We have to recognize that the moment we take hold of anything, we place everything in a world of surfaces. This in itself is not a problem, but then we confuse what we've grasped—what we think, believe, or imagine—with Reality itself. We confuse our thoughts, opinions, and beliefs with actual Knowledge. This is where our deepest suffering comes from.

Through realization, a bodhisattva comes into this world in *this moment,* with no desire for acquiring the right idea or explanation about how things are. The bodhisattva realizes in that moment that nothing is anything in particular—including the bodhisattva, "me."

We all come into the world again and again and again— now as a pedestrian, now as a reader, now as a bodhisattva, now as something else equally temporal and fluid and ineffable.

The bodhisattva comes into the world with this understanding. There's no reaching for the superficial, no grasping at frozen forms, no attempt to embrace the temporary expedient of knowing accordingly.

Forsaking understanding and forsaking being understood involve not being caught up with thought. Thus we enter into each situation undefined and undefiled—not as a particular thing, not as an ego, not with a personal agenda, not with expectations that our sensibilities and desires should be honored.

And in forsaking understanding and being understood, there's a lack of agitation, discomfort, and nervousness. It isn't troubling that knowing accordingly is absent.

A reliance on knowing accordingly inevitably creates agitation in the mind. Indeed, we can *see* the profound disturbance that arises whenever we reach for something graspable, such as an idea or an explanation or an answer. This is the most profound expression of *dukkha*—the basis of all suffering.

Ultimately there's nothing to grasp. If we really understand that this is how the world is, how it's always been, and how it always will and must be, then we can move beyond the discomfort of not knowing accordingly—the very discomfort that commonly keeps us from *seeing* Reality.

Most of us want something to grasp, something to hold on to, something to understand, something beneath our feet. We think we need this, and we feel very uncomfortable with the thought that whatever we've put under our feet doesn't work and isn't Truth. And so we reach for the next thing and the next.

Yet none of the things we put beneath our feet ever holds up. It can't.

Nevertheless, in each moment, *here we are.*

Truth and Reality are always here for us to *see*. We don't need to stand on any particular idea, belief, answer, or other mental structure. In each moment we can *see* what's actually going on without grasping—without needing to find something to bolster or comfort us. After all, what is there to bolster? What's being threatened?

We spend a great deal of time and energy fearing and worrying. We're driven in all kinds of ways because we think we have something we need to please and protect and support.

The bodhisattva comes into the world without needing any of this.

In *this moment* it's possible to realize that we do not need to understand, to be understood, to have the right idea. All we need to do is awaken to *here* and *now*—to stop jabbering to ourselves and be present in *this moment*.

There's nothing to prove, nothing to figure out, nothing to get, nothing to understand. When we finally stop explaining everything to ourselves, we may discover that in silence, complete understanding was *here* all along.

34

HOW DO WE KNOW?

WHEN WE FIRST approach Buddhist teachings, they often seem very complicated. To many people, they may also seem arcane, foreign, and confusing.

But what the Buddha taught is actually quite simple and immediate if we stick to the original teachings. It's just that we are complicated. We think too much.

The essential point of the Buddhadharma is simply to wake up to Reality.

I've been told that Buddhism teaches three ways by which we can *know* Truth: one, from authority; two, by logical deduction; and three, through direct experience. I've never, however, seen such a statement in any Buddhist text. And whether this is a Buddhist teaching or not, it's fundamentally flawed.

If we look carefully, we'll notice that the first two approaches will quickly unravel and crumble into dust. Direct experience also unravels, but instead of crumbling to dust, it completely disappears, leaving no trace whatsoever.

If this seems complicated, arcane, foreign, or confusing, please keep reading. Soon you'll see the simplicity in it.

Let's first look at the idea of arriving at Knowledge by way of authority. This approach is easily dismantled. In fact, the British philosopher Bertrand Russell dismissed it in a single sentence when he noted that the problem with authority is that you can always find another authority to oppose it.

The foremost authority in Buddhism is supposedly the Buddha himself. Yet the Buddha explicitly encouraged people *not* to rely on the authority of others, including him. The Buddha often made remarks like, "Don't believe me just because others do or because you see me as your teacher." He continually admonished people to look carefully in order to *see* and *know* for themselves. This means neither blindly accepting the words of some external authority nor rejecting them out of hand but listening to them and testing them against actual experience.

As the Dalai Lama once put it, "There are many things we Buddhists should learn from the latest scientific findings. And scientists can learn from Buddhist explanations. We must conduct research and then accept the results. If they don't stand up to experimentation, Buddha's own words must be rejected."

This is very much in keeping with what the Buddha taught as well as with the modern scientific method.

We sometimes have the mistaken notion that enlightened people, once they *see* Reality, are able to speak of the Absolute with words that are Absolute as well. Then we can write down their utterances and preserve, study, and revere them for all time. But we humans—enlightened or not—never experience absolutes. We experience change. This is what the Buddha taught, and it applies to his teaching as well.

This is why some Buddhist groups get together periodically to examine what they're doing, what works, what still fits, and what does not. Because times change, what might have been appropriate in a different time and place may no longer work *here* and *now*. We need not—and should not—lock ourselves in a frame that made sense twenty-five hundred years ago in some foreign culture (or even twenty years ago here). Some of it might not apply to us today or might even be downright harmful.

We must continuously reexamine what we teach. We need to ask, "Is this effective? Is this conducive to helping people open their eyes?"

In short, as the Buddha taught, while everything is to be viewed and handled with utmost respect, nothing is—or can be—sacred. This was why the Buddha likened his teaching to a raft, which should be left behind once the river has been crossed.

One other point about authority: no human being or institution ever has more authority than that granted by other human beings. This means that *you* are the final authority in terms of whom you give credence to and how you live your life.

Turning over this authority to anyone else is a kind of spiritual laziness. You'll be disinclined to pay careful and critical attention to what's actually going on, and you'll be left wide open to being manipulated, misled, and scammed.

The Buddha recognized this and warned against it. For instance, he told people not to make any images of him. (And people didn't at first.)

You need to realize that *you* are Buddha. Yet the more we glorify and deify the man we call the Buddha, the more difficult it is for us to wake up. After all, if you make your teachers into gods, how can you realize the Truth that you are fundamentally no different from them?

In the end, it comes down to this: authority, which is yours already, rests only with direct experience. Ultimately, there is no other place for you to look.

The second means by which we can supposedly *know* Truth is through logical deduction. Certainly this is a more valuable and useful tool than blind obedience. It can keep us on track so that we don't come to conclusions that don't follow from our original assumptions. But logical deduction can tell us nothing about the validity of our original premises. Thus, in and of itself, logical deduction can't be relied upon to bring us to Truth.

Here's an example of a perfectly legitimate logical form called a syllogism:

All birds are green.
The King of Spain is a bird.
Therefore, the King of Spain is green.

The logic here is flawless. Since, however, both of the initial premises are false (not to mention absurd), we arrive at a conclusion that's perfectly consistent with the premises but false (not to mention ridiculous). The tool of logic functioned perfectly, but we need something else to ensure that the basic premises are valid.

Actually, in Buddhist teachings we do use logic. We use it to show that our commonly accepted premises about Reality are false or flawed. Buddhist logic, such as the logic employed by Nagarjuna, brings us to a point of *seeing* that all our concepts leave us dangling in space at the end of a rope. Eventually, after trying out a variety of ropes, we *see* that when we rely on our thoughts and concepts, all we'll ever be led to are free-floating tethers. We *see* that this method will never get us to Truth.

Let's pause for a moment and take stock of where we are. We can't rely on authority, and we can't rely on mere logical deduction. Neither is sufficient to direct us to Truth. Thus we can only rely on direct experience.

After authority and logic have both unraveled and crumbled to dust, and even after all our concepts—of self, of other, of wisdom, of Emptiness, of Buddhism—have all faded and blown away, direct experience is still operating. It doesn't go away. And careful observation of actual experience reveals something else: direct experience does not supply an experiencer.

Hui Neng, the sixth ancestor of Zen, asked another monk, Huai-jang, "Where do you come from?"

"I come from Tung-shan," said Huai-jang.

"What is it that thus comes?" asked Hui Neng.

Huai-jang was speechless. For eight long years he pondered the question; then one day it dawned upon him, and he exclaimed, "Even to say it *is* something doesn't hit the mark."

We need to *see* this for ourselves, directly. On close examination, whatever we claim as our self immediately disintegrates. And yet direct experience keeps rolling on.

We never actually experience things "out there." And we never actually experience an experiencer "in here." We only *think* we do.

We're all born into this world naked and innocent. We have nothing to go on but what's happening—direct experience. Just *this*.

The problem is that most of us don't really know how to attend to actual experience very well. The reason is simple: we think too much.

Yet attending to actual experience is simple. We only need to start looking and note how what we *see* differs from what we think. We need to confront paradox and confusion.

I'm not talking about vague, mystical notions here. Start looking carefully at trees, rocks, birds, people, mind, thought, feeling, even imaginary things like angels and hungry ghosts. Look at them all as experience rather than as substantive things "out there," removed from "you." Calmly and quietly (that is, with no mental dialogue), just watch what's going on. This is a simple, straightforward activity. It's not arcane, foreign, complicated, or confusing.

Continuously examine what you're doing, what you're thinking, what you're saying. Observe what you believe, what you say. Do this over and over again, without supposing that a time will ever come when this activity will stop. Let logic and authority drop away under their own weight.

What remains is what has been *right here* all along: Reality, before we try to make something of it.

35

NOTHING ELSE

Walt Whitman, in the opening lines of the thirty-second part of his longest poem, *Song of Myself*, wrote:

> I think I could turn and live with the animals, they're so
>   placid and self-contain'd,
> I stand and look at them long and long.
>
> They do not sweat and whine about their condition,
> They do not lie awake in the dark and weep for their sins,
> They do not make me sick discussing their duty to God,
> Not one is dissatisfied, not one is demented with the mania
>   of owning things,
> Not one kneels to another, nor to his kind that lived
>   thousands of years ago,
> Not one is respectable or unhappy over the whole earth.

As Whitman points out, animals are self-contained. They don't look to anything outside of *just this*. Each comes fully equipped to be a cat or a cow, a lion or a deer, a bird or a fish. They're ready and willing to sleep, breed, find food and shelter, and survive.

Therein lies their serenity. They don't act with leaning minds. Without looking outside themselves, they live entirely in the moment. Even as the lion kills the deer, the world rolls on; all is placid and serene.

Animals are artless—without guile or deceit. They don't try to manipulate our impressions of them or cover up the truth about themselves.

The same is true of a human baby. A newborn shows no sign of feeling separate from the world. Sometimes just noticing this quality in a baby (or in an animal) is enough to give us grown-ups a momentary sense of lightness and freedom.

But why can't we live with such peace and serenity ourselves? What's our problem?

Our problem is that we earnestly believe that there's something outside ourselves that we need to get to make ourselves whole. We believe that what will really satisfy the ache of our hearts is "out there" somewhere. So we go about trying to satisfy our innermost want by going "out there," hunting for that something as if it were prey.

Seeking and getting are what we're used to, what we understand. We're so used to getting material things that we assume that what we need spiritually can be acquired in the same way.

Yet this very way of approaching Reality is what traps us. As Thoreau pointed out, possessions are more easily acquired than gotten rid of. And often they only burden and disturb us and leave us wanting ever more.

But satisfying the deep need of the heart is not a matter of getting something.

If we could put aside our petty wants and examine our actual needs, we might discover what we truly do need and want. We might also *see* that these real needs are easy to satisfy. We'd *see* that we, too, like animals, are self-contained. There's nothing "out there" we need to acquire. The world is always *here*. Reality is forever at hand. What we want and need is ours already.

I have a dear friend who, when we were kids, had a small dog. He named her Tippy because she was all black except for the very tip of her tail, which was white. Tippy was well trained and very disciplined. We'd often go on hikes with Tippy, and she'd always respond to my friend's commands.

By the time we were in high school, Tippy was getting white in the face and mellowing with age. She developed arthritis and had a lot of pain, though she never complained. Eventually she developed cancer in her jaw and face and couldn't eat. But still she did not whine or complain about her condition.

The time came when my friend realized Tippy had to be euthanized. He went to get Tippy for the last time. As he came into the room, Tippy was too weak to lift her head, though she tried. But her tail started to wag. She was happy to see her friend and master. Even as she faced death, she was serene.

Unlike animals, we fool ourselves about death. We think we know that we're going to die. But death isn't something we *can know* as an idea. What we call "death" is only something we imagine. Real death—Real anything—is always *right here, right now.* It's not lurking somewhere off in the future. It occurs—it can only occur—*now.*

Animals are not confused about this matter. It is we, with our complex thoughts, who are confused, we who whine about our condition. We do this because we imagine everything set apart from ourselves, *here* and *now.*

But what you or I or anyone thinks doesn't belong to *now.* It's not the Reality we actually live from moment to moment.

Birth and death occur *right here, right now.* Were we to awaken to *this moment,* we'd find nothing to complain about.

36

IT'S NOT A MATTER
OF BELIEF

BUDDHISM DOESN'T REQUIRE a belief in God or in a holy scripture to be taken on faith. In fact, the Buddha-dharma is not about believing things at all. It's a religious tradition that dates back twenty-five hundred years, but it's not a belief system.

Indeed, any teaching or practice or tradition designed to draw our attention to Truth cannot be based in belief. It can't be about buying into concepts. It can only be about examining, testing, and *knowing* the actual, immediate, direct experience of *this moment*.

Most of us approach the big questions of life by putting together a set of ideas and beliefs in our minds and then relying on those ideas and beliefs to explain everything to ourselves. We do this in an attempt to make sense of ourselves and of the world.

But as you may have realized already, we can't make sense of the world through these means. Our beliefs and ideas simply won't support their own weight, let alone our weight and the weight of the world. This is why, if we lumber through life trying to make sense of experience by holding to our beliefs, our concepts, our models of Reality, then deep down we'll feel insecure and confused.

This doesn't mean that we can't or shouldn't have beliefs. When it comes to getting along from day to day, we can't help but have a wide variety of beliefs. Most of us believe it's best to obey traffic laws and to practice good hygiene. Beliefs such as these are functional and often necessary.

But when it comes to the big questions—"How did I get here?" "Where am I going?" "What is reality?" "What's life all about?"—the stories we come up with to supply us with answers fall short. While they may comfort us for a time, ultimately they will only lead us to pain and confusion simply because whatever we tell ourselves must always remain dubious.

We need to recognize that there's something wrong with such questions in the first place. We need to *see* that they come out of our mental constructs—our egoistic desires, fears, and speculations—rather than out of direct experience, out of *just seeing*.

Only by learning to recognize such confusion within our own thinking can we stop embroiling ourselves further. But the ways we embroil ourselves are varied and subtle.

At Dharma Field, the Buddhist meditation and learning center where I teach, you won't find a buddha statue. It's not that it's wrong or bad to have a buddha statue in a meditation hall or at a Buddhist center, but it can needlessly confuse a lot of us by inciting us to create a wide range of notions and emotions about it. Some people think "idol worship" and are repelled by it. Others fall in love with it and want to get one of their own right away. Either way, such reactions are not conducive to waking up.

So, instead, we just have a large stone in our meditation hall. It's hard (though not impossible) to have a lot of ideas about it. It's just a stone.

Nevertheless, every bit as much as a buddha statue (or anything else we might put there), it expresses Truth.

We found it in a field west of town, right where glaciers left it tens of thousands of years ago. It originally formed in ancient mountains, which long ago washed away.

Though it's fairly plain, it looks appropriate in the meditation hall. Sitting quietly, it expresses stability elegantly. Yet it doesn't disturb anyone because it doesn't look like anyone's idea of a buddha (or anyone's idea of anything—except perhaps a stone).

Even so, the stone—and the fleeting flower that sits beside it—help us put our little lives into perspective. As we all sit together in the meditation hall, our lives appear to unfold at a pace in between the lives of the long-lived stone and the fleeting flower.

The stone is a natural object—made without motive. Thus it portrays the qualities of a buddha, along with stillness, calmness, centeredness, patience, tolerance—even magnanimity, compassion, and wisdom. The stone, just sitting still, reminds us of our true nature, before we stir our minds in thought. Yet all the while, remaining a natural object, it offends no one and encourages no particular belief or thought.

But why have anything at all? This is an option, of course. But in each moment something has to manifest. Some form will appear. That things form in our world of this and that is necessary. That we must grasp them, however, is not.

For this reason alone, it's best that the forms we create are not too elaborate. It's easy for us to quickly build form upon form upon form until we no longer know what we're doing or why. We're so easily caught by forms we begin to think that certain forms are not only Real but also necessary and vital.

On the other hand, if we try somehow to drop forms completely, we deceive ourselves. No matter what we do, a form will still appear. Even in this formless world, form always appears. Indeed, it's only in this world of Emptiness that forms *can* appear.

Whatever we do, however we live, there will always be an atmosphere, an aroma, a flavor to our life and to our experience in *this moment*. But Zen is about not getting caught by this or that form, this or that belief.

Though people and circumstances continuously pull in different directions, we have to *look* at what we ourselves are actually doing. We need to *see* what's taking place within our own heart and mind. We need to *see* what we cling to, what we insist upon, what we're fearful of losing. Over and over, we need to bring ourselves back to what we're doing—*now*, in *this moment.*

What disturbs, frightens, and confuses us is our thought, our beliefs—what we form in our minds. In particular, it's those notions that are expressed mainly in terms of our own ego. This is how we unwittingly entangle ourselves in realities and matters of little or no consequence; this is what keeps us mired in ignorance and confusion.

We only need to *see* that this is so and thus break free immediately.

PART THREE

PURELY MIND

37

HOW TO BE LIBERATED
ON THE SPOT

T HE GREAT EIGHTH-CENTURY Chinese Zen teacher Baizhang once said that if you could realize that there is no connection between your senses and the outside world, you would be liberated on the spot.

This seems strange to most of us. We think that there's a world out there, a world we take in through the gates of our senses. For each of us, it appears as though "I myself am in here, getting readings on a world that is out there. I can see it. I can hear it. I can smell it, taste it, and touch it." We feel this sense of separateness quite strongly. But where does this feeling come from?

This feeling is consciousness itself. Simply put, consciousness is an awareness of an object (in this case, what we call the outside world) as well as an awareness of a subject (in this case, what we call me, in here). But both the object and the subject—as separate, discrete entities—are mental constructions. In actual experience, there is no boundary between a "here" and a "there," between what I call me and what I designate as the external world. Both subject and object are illusions created by Mind.

There's a Zen aphorism that says, "Whatever comes in through the gates is foreign." The gates are the senses, and whatever we believe comes in through them seems separate from us, foreign to us. But that's only because we've created a conceptual split between what we call our senses and what we call the outside world.

Baizhang correctly points out that there's no connection between our senses and an external world. To see a connection implies that we have a twoness—me in here, and the world out there—that in some way can be connected. But Baizhang tells us that this twoness isn't what is really happening.

Reality is always right *here*, right *now*. It's just *this*—vibrant, immediate experience. *This* doesn't come in through any gates. How can it if it isn't outside in the first place? It's intimate. It's already Mind itself. We may call *this* experience "airplane" or "bird" or "love" or "fear," but in Reality, it's just *this* arising in Mind.

Most of the time, however, we superimpose something onto what is immediate and Real. We project onto what we directly experience, and we extend that projection through time and space. Thus we create subject and objects. And then, in relation to these objects, longings and loathings arise in our mind.

Thus we mistake the world that we've created in our minds and projected "out there" with Reality.

The upshot is that we don't engage the world as it actually is. Instead, we react to the world as we assume it to be—or, worse, as we think or wish it ought to be. We live out our lives in our imaginations, reacting to our concepts of the world rather than attending to actual, directly perceived Reality.

In spite of this, the fact is that you do *see* the world exactly as the awakened *see* it, all the time. There isn't any difference between what the enlightened *see* and what we all *see*. Perception is the same for all of us. But the awakened stay with perception rather than reject it in favor of their mental constructions and ideas about reality.

Though it manifests in countless forms, Reality is only one way—it could not be otherwise. And all who *see*, *see* the same thing.

It's not that the world of multiplicity we see all around us isn't real. It's not that the plane overhead is a phantom, or that the page you're reading doesn't exist. It's all real enough. But if we think this realm of objects and subject is the full explanation of Reality, then we quickly become lost in a world of confusion, of wanting, of craving, and of fearing. It's a difficult life, though we might not fully realize it.

What we have to *see* is that this very same reality can be viewed in a completely different way, a way based on perception alone.

The awakened *see* Reality as it is. They *see* that enlightenment is nothing more than not being deceived by the conceptual world each of us creates.

Consciousness splits the world into this and that and the next thing. The most basic split, of course, is "here I am" and "out there is everything else." But when we understand what consciousness is and how it functions, we realize that our sense of self and other, of subject and object, is an illusion created by consciousness itself.

The enlightened person isn't taken in by such conceptual dualities. Still, it isn't that the illusion goes away. The illusion still appears, but it's *seen* for what it is—an illusion. And this *seeing* is utterly liberating.

As the Buddha put it, "Just as a man steps upon a serpent and shudders in fear but then looks down and notices that it's only a rope, so it was that one day I realized that what I was calling 'I' cannot be found, and all fear and anxiety vanished with my mistake."

But what, exactly, has changed? In a sense, nothing. "The rope" is still "there"; "the foot" is still "there." But everything is *seen* as empty of self. Thus with *seeing*, the sense of "I" drops away. We no longer have to get in there and manipulate or control.

Enlightened people don't suddenly disappear. Neither do they suddenly forget how to eat a meal or drive a car or take care of their children. But they understand that they cannot hurt others without doing injury to themselves. In the end, what is understood is that *this* is all of one fabric.

One of the great moral questions in the Bible is when Cain murders his brother, Abel. God comes to Cain and asks, "Where is your brother?" And Cain replies, "Am I my brother's keeper?" How can we answer a question like this? If we remain caught by our conceptualizing minds, it's impossible because it demands an answer that cannot be mentally formulated. For how can we be our brother's keeper without controlling him? And if we are not his keeper, why do we feel for him when his house burns to the ground or he's starving or he's unjustly held against his will?

But what if you realized—in your bones and in your guts— that there was ultimately no way of distinguishing between yourself and your brother? What if you *saw* that "I'm here and he's there" isn't a full explanation of Reality? What if you *saw* that injury to your brother is injury to yourself? With this direct awareness of Reality, the dilemma dissolves.

Your experience is always *this*, right *here*, right *now*. There's no separate outside world, no separate senses, and therefore no connection between them. How can there be a connection between something and itself?

38

THIS WILL NEVER
COME AGAIN

AFTER A BRISK WALK on a cold winter day, I settled before the fire and opened my volume of Emily Dickinson. The first line my gaze fell upon was this: "That it will never come again."

I was ready for it, and so I began to read:

> *That it will never come again*
> *Is what makes life so sweet.*
> *Believing what we don't believe*
> *Does not exhilarate.*
>
> *That if it be, it be at best*
> *An ablative estate—*
> *This instigates an appetite*
> *Precisely opposite.*

Emily Dickinson's poem touches the deep longing in the human heart to live forever. We don't want to die. We don't want to pass out of existence.

At first glance, the line *That it will never come again* would seem to sum up our culture's general understanding of our life. But surely Buddhists think differently. We don't just go around once: we're born again and again and again—and this just goes on and on. Isn't this how we're supposed to understand life as Buddhists?

No. This is basically the same as thinking that we'll live forever. This is not what the Buddha taught at all. It's just another form of eternalism.

Dogen Zenji, the great Japanese Zen teacher, said that just as firewood does not return to firewood once it is burned, so a person does not return to life after death. So what about this matter of being born again and again? What does it mean to be reborn? And what, exactly, is Emily Dickinson writing about?

She's writing about *just this*. *This* wonderful, clear, bright, blue winter day. It won't come again. There will be other, very similar days, no doubt. But *this day* will not return. And you sitting here reading this, you will not sit again in this same way, with these same thoughts and feelings. None of this will ever be the same again. Even as you set down this book and leave the room, you'll not be the person who walked in. *This* will never come again. This is always the case.

That *this* will never come again is what it actually means to be born again and again. We, and indeed the whole world, are born repeatedly, over and over, in each new moment.

But there's a caveat. This change, this flux, is complete and thorough. So thorough, in fact, that there's nothing solid—no "we"—*here* at all. There's nothing solid that returns or endures. There's no "I" in this picture. And no "world outside me," either.

When we think in terms of reincarnation, we're thinking in terms of a self. We're seeing everything in terms of "me" persisting through time. "And when I die," we say, "I'll come back. I'll be born again as someone else." But this is absurd. We can't possibly be "someone else." How can you be someone other than who you are in *this* moment? How can anything be other than what it is *now?*

Such thoughts are nothing more (or less) than the profound longing in the human heart for persistence—when in fact, nothing in the world persists.

Nevertheless, this wonderful, precious, brilliant moment appears *now, now, now,* and again *now,* reborn again and again, moment after moment. It's forever *just this,* yet with no one moment ever to come again. This, says Emily Dickinson, "Is what makes life so sweet."

What makes human life—which is inseparable from *this moment*—so precious is its fleeting nature. And not merely that it doesn't last but that it never returns. This is the actual vibrant life we experience and *know* directly. Yet it is enough.

In this poem Dickinson has a very curious set of lines: *Believing what we don't believe / Does not exhilarate.* What is it that we believe but don't believe?

We believe in permanence. At least, we'd like to. We long for permanence in our hearts precisely because, underneath our superficial thoughts and convictions, we can't really believe in it.

Whether we admit it to ourselves or not, we *see* nothing but this boundless transitoriness. Life shows us nothing but flux and flow and change and movement. Every cell and atom of our bodies, every thought and feeling of our minds, is flux. Nothing holds still or endures, even for a moment. We cannot find permanence in anything. Yet we carry on—in fact, we construct our lives—as though this were not so.

Yet beneath it all, we *know* we don't believe.

We envision a permanent oasis, a heavenly abode—our Pure Land, our Elysian Field—and despair because we never find it. It's never *here*, and *here* is all we've ever *known*.

But if we fully digest our innermost understanding— that the world reveals nothing to us but thoroughgoing change— we will *see* that *here* is precisely where we belong and where we need to be. And then we can appreciate that this world of Emptiness is vibrant and alive precisely *because* nothing endures.

What we would freeze and hold close, as if to quiet the ache of the heart, is transitoriness itself. It doesn't occur to us that, beyond the impossibility of ever succeeding in making solidity out of Emptiness, we don't need to hold on to the world. We don't need to make anything extra out of the aching in our hearts. So instead of longing and reaching for what never was and never will be, we can awaken to the thoroughgoing impermanence of *this moment*.

To live our lives as though there were some end point is to live in fear of that end point. The thought of arriving at some final destination where everything is fine—or where everything somehow stops or repeats itself—is to deny this world where nothing stays put. It's to deny life and consciousness itself.

In believing what we don't believe, we live life with the brakes on—without exhilaration. Yet vitality springs from letting go of any concern for what sustains us. This vitality is found only in living life in accord with actual experience, unhindered by our wishes, speculations, and beliefs.

If we would just dig a little deeper into actual experience and step aside from our constructed realities and from the longed-for objects of our thoughts and imaginations, we'd find life as it's actually lived.

But as it's actually lived, as Emily Dickinson says, it's at best an *ablative estate*. That is, it's continuously receding from us. We can't grasp it.

And so, Dickinson tells us, *This instigates an appetite / Precisely opposite*. It's this very way of imagining the world—coming out of a deep desire to hold to a self that we hope can endure in some pleasant abode—that instigates in us an appetite that's precisely the opposite of life. We want the good, the wonderful, the pleasant—but we want it embalmed forever.

Whatever we take hold of, if we pursue it long enough, only points to meaninglessness. And so we fear there might be only meaninglessness. But the feeling of meaninglessness would never arise if we would not reach for what is not there.

What we truly need—and already have—cannot be dreamed of or even wished for. It's called the Wishless. The Signless. And it looks and feels exactly like *this*.

39

THE ELIXIR
OF IMMORTALITY

WHEN THE BUDDHA was asked to sum up his teaching in a single word, he said, "Awareness."

This Awareness the Buddha spoke of is not an awareness of particular things, thoughts, or feelings. It's Awareness itself—before things, thoughts, and feelings appear.

This is also the Awareness the Buddha spoke of when he said, "Awareness is the path to the deathless. Ignorance is the path of death. Those who are *aware* do not die; those who are ignorant are as if dead already."

Human beings suffer from confusion, from fear, from longing, from loathing. The main problem we suffer from is that we know we're going to die. This registers deeply within the human psyche. It's very painful to contemplate because it's something we don't want to face.

When we awaken to the fact that we have this problem called death, it leaves us wondering: What meaning is there in life? What satisfaction is there if in the end it all comes to naught? There's nothing we can make or create that doesn't pass away. Thus we become baffled and frightened.

When the Buddha spoke of Awareness as "the path to the deathless," he wasn't just using a figure of speech. He was pointing to what's actually going on. He was directing our attention to something we can't believe, grasp, take hold of, or conceptualize in any way. Still, we can learn to *see* what he was getting at.

"The Song of the Jewel Mirror Awareness," a poem by the great Chinese Zen teacher Tung-shan, speaks of the very same Awareness that the Buddha pointed to.

This image of a jewel mirror was used as a way to express the source from which all things issue. All the myriad things, thoughts, and feelings we experience appear like images in a mirror: vivid yet insubstantial. The ungraspable mirror is what's Real, while the seemingly isolated things that appear in it are not.

Consider, for example, the simple act of smelling a rose. We see the rose, feel the rose, bring it close, breathe in through our nose. We "smell the rose," as we say, though this refers more to how we conceptualize our experience than it does to what is actually experienced. To say we smell a *fragrance* would be closer to the actual experience.

But where does the act of smelling a fragrance take place? If we attend carefully, we can *see* that all of our usual accounts of the experience start to break down.

Is the fragrance in the rose? If it was, how could you smell it? You're *here* while the rose is "out there" somewhere. On the other hand, if the rose were removed, you surely wouldn't smell the fragrance. But if *you* were removed—or if the air in between you and the rose were removed—you also wouldn't smell it.

So is the fragrance in the rose? Is it in your nose? Is it in the air in between? Is it in the air if no one is around to smell it? If so, how could we tell?

Is the fragrance in your brain, then? And if it's in your brain, then why is the rose necessary at all?

Ultimately, the simple act of "smelling a rose"—or any other act involving a subject and object—becomes impossible to pin down and utterly insubstantial.

Gradually, however, we can begin to appreciate what the experience of smelling a rose actually entails. It's of the nature of the mirror itself—that is, that the source of *all* experience is Mind. As such, the act of smelling—or seeing or hearing or touching or thinking—literally has no location. This non-locality is the very essence of Mind.

We naively think Mind conveys actual objects to us, as though the objects themselves were Real. Although they may appear this way, no separate objects are ever created and conveyed to us. In fact, such an arrangement is quite literally impossible.

We know from physics, for example, that the book you're holding and the hand that holds it are reconstructed (that is, reborn) moment after moment as a blur of rapidly moving molecules and atoms, each exchanging electrons and energy with other molecules and atoms at enormous speed. As a result, in no two instants is there the same book or hand. The whole picture reduces to energy and movement.

Early Buddhist teachers, who did not have the benefit of modern physics, nevertheless recognized this as total, thoroughgoing impermanence. Nothing whatsoever abides for a moment. In each instant we find a different picture, a changed universe.

And why is the physical world this way? Because this is the only way it *can* be experienced. It's a mental experience. Mind is the Source.

But I'm not talking about our common idea of mind, like "your mind" or "my mind." Your mind and my mind are just more examples of the mentally fabricated and labeled stuff, such as "this book," "the rose," "the fragrance," and all the rest. These all exhibit a reality we cannot deny; yet if we think they are all there is to Reality, we've got it all backward. The multitude of labeled things is not Reality but merely our interpretation—our concepts—of Reality.

All of philosophy sprouted from the conviction that there must surely be a way to live, a way to understand human life, a way to conduct our affairs, that doesn't lead to suffering. This is the basic problem for us human beings, and we have looked for a solution for millennia. We've devised philosophies of all kinds—not to mention religions, political theories, and so forth—all in this great endeavor to resolve the problem of human suffering. And yet suffering and ignorance just go on and on. What's the problem?

When we search for the pure land, the place of peace, the right philosophy, the ultimate abode, or whatever, believing there's really something "out there" waiting to be found, we set ourselves up for disappointment. There isn't any such thing. But as long as we keep thinking in such terms, we're headed for either of two destinations. Either we remain naive and callow or we become grim, crusty, and cynical.

We overlook that this all comes about because of our thought. As long as we hold to anything at all, doubt and despair will fester deeply in our minds.

But this despair only comes about because we've locked on to the notion that there has to be some wonderful, perfect, healing object or concept or philosophy or answer in the first place. And since there isn't, we react as though human life has no meaning.

As long as we're stuck in this place, there appears no way to resolve this profound human problem. Either we're ultimately doomed to realize that we live in a meaningless universe or we're doomed to abandon our intellect and live in a fool's paradise. Both of these are forms of hell.

Is there any other option outside of these two terrible extremes?

Consider what another ancient Chinese Zen teacher, Baizhang, spoke of as the "elixir of immortality." An elixir is a medicine that cures all ills. The elixir that Baizhang refers to is pure, naked, objectless Awareness.

To Baizhang, we suffer because we buy in to the notion of substance. That is, we think that the things we see, hear, smell, taste, touch, and think are real, solid, and enduring. But naked, objectless Awareness reveals to us a very different Reality.

In speaking of the elixir of immortality, Baizhang is speaking not just figuratively or poetically; he's speaking of the Awareness that nothing really dies—and that nothing is ever born.

To the extent that this is *seen*, our experience of the world is utterly transformed. And virtually all that we suffer from—confusion, pain, longing and loathing, loss and sorrow, fear of death—comes to an end. Indeed, it doesn't even arise anymore because we're no longer looking "out there" for anything that will satisfy. We can *see* that there is no "out there"—and no "in here."

There are different ways of looking at this elixir of immortality—this realization that nothing dies—but I'll give just two examples.

First, we could look to Nagarjuna's observation that nothing is impermanent.

When we first hear this, it probably strikes us as very strange, perhaps even contrary to Buddhist teachings. After all, impermanence is a basic tenet of the Buddhadharma. And it makes so much sense. It seems glaringly obvious, once it's pointed out, that nothing lasts. Yet Nagarjuna says that a complete and thorough understanding of impermanence is that nothing is impermanent.

What Nagarjuna is pointing to is that believing things are impermanent involves a contradiction. First we posit separate, persisting things (in effect, absolute objects); then we refer to them as impermanent (that is, relative). What we fail to *see* is that we are still holding to a view of substance. We don't really appreciate the thoroughgoing nature of change, the thoroughgoing nature of selflessness.

Nagarjuna makes it abundantly clear that impermanence (the relative) is total, complete, thoroughgoing, Absolute. It's not that the universe is made up of innumerable objects in flux. There's *only* flux. Nothing is (or can be) riding along in the flux, like a cork in a stream; nothing actually arises or passes away. There's *only* stream.

Another way of looking at this realization that nothing dies comes from Bodhidharma, the first Zen ancestor in China. Commenting on the Buddhist precept of not taking life, he said, "Not nursing a view of extinction is called the precept of not killing." In other words, to hold a view that something actually dies or passes away is to believe that there are actual, abiding entities that come into and go out of existence.

That forms appear to come and go cannot be denied. But to assume the existence of imaginary persisting entities and attach them to these apparent comings and goings is delusion.

When the Buddha said that those who are ignorant live as though dead already, he was saying that when we imagine permanence within the forms that appear to come and go, we necessarily live with fear, confusion, and the sense that human life is ultimately meaningless. It's a huge burden to bear—and it all comes from our marvelous ability to abstract our experience into things and thoughts. It's a grand illusion that easily takes us in—and we are left trembling in our boots at the thought that we will die, that everything else will also pass out of existence (at least for us), and, worst of all, that we really don't understand anything. Thus we miss the field and fabric of *just this*—dynamic Reality itself. We are, in the Buddha's words, "as if dead already."

One other image in Buddhist texts is used to express this objectless Awareness that nothing dies. It's called the Golden Fish. It's not a typical image of something we can grasp. In fact, the term is used for something we can't even imagine.

We don't know what it is because it's nothing in particular. It's not an object at all. In fact, it's not even anything we can name, let alone possess or form a relationship with. Yet it's what will truly satisfy.

But, since it has no location, there's nothing we can do to find it. All we need to do is lower the net.

40

ICE FORMING IN FIRE

D OGEN ZENJI said, "What is Reality? An icicle forming in fire."

"This seems impossible," my own teacher, Jikai Dainin, once
observed. "Nevertheless, this is Reality. We live it every day."

Dogen is not simply using a beautiful, poetic metaphor
here. He's pointing directly to the actual experience of *this
moment*. This is precisely how Reality is manifested in our lives
from moment to moment—as ice forming in fire.

Consider memory, for example. Whenever I ask people
what part of their mental experience is most enduring, usually
they say it's their memories. But the reliability and stability of
memory are highly questionable.

Recently I revisited Itasca State Park, at the headwaters of
the Mississippi River. I vividly remember traveling there with
my family when I was a boy. I also have a clear and detailed
memory of jumping across the Mississippi near where it
spills out of Lake Itasca to start its long course to the Gulf of

Mexico. I remember distinctly the banks on either side of what was really a creek, not a river, with tufts of grass hanging over the clear water as it flowed out of the lake. And I clearly remember jumping from one bank to the other.

Clear or not, however, my memory is wrong.

When I returned there recently, I saw my error immediately. Much of what I remembered was still in place and was very much as I remembered it—the grassy, tufted banks, the log footbridge, the historical marker. But the river was much wider than I had remembered. There was no way I could have jumped across.

The fact is that our memories are not at all the sound, enduring reports we take them to be. They get stitched together with other thoughts and things and are modified over time. Thus we can have clear, distinct memories that are inaccurate or even wholly false. Even shared memories offer no guarantee of their reliability.

Memories are like icicles that form in the fiery flow of our thoughts. They seem solidly formed and enduring amid all our changes of mood and the constant pileup of our experiences and concepts. We carry them with us for years, not noticing that they've lost pieces and had new pieces sewn in.

Our memories are just another way we've constructed the world in order to hold it in our mind. They have the look of solidity—they seem real, discrete, unchanged, and enduring—but they do change, just like every other formed thing.

The fact is, nothing holds still. It's all flux. In this respect, memories are no different from any other aspect of Reality.

The same is true of our emotional life, or indeed any other aspect of our mind that we may want to consider.

Yet we continue to think of people as being particular ways—good or bad, happy or sad, generous or stingy, friendly or threatening. Though everything about that person has changed, we don't see it because the objects of our minds become like icicles—brittle and inflexible—and we pay attention to those frozen objects instead of to Reality.

First we freeze out our own lives and the lives of our contemporaries in this way, then we transmit our frozen notions from generation to generation, thus dragging countless innocent people—our children and their descendants—into our folly.

In many parts of the world, people are taught hatreds that look back hundreds of years. Though no one alive today really knows how the fighting began, people create or revise memories and stories to justify continuing the conflicts. Thus we perpetuate violence, sorrow, and misery not only for ourselves but for posterity as well.

All our warring has been a legacy of thought and belief. It has come directly out of the frozen constructs of our minds—as though all our ideas, beliefs, and memories were real and needed to be acted on. We would do well to forget about how we think or believe or remember or imagine things used to be and instead look at how we're carrying on in the present moment. *This* is where we're going to come to our senses.

. . .

We create icicles not just out of memories. We do it in every moment, with all the objects, thoughts, and feelings that appear in our minds.

Consider a whirlpool. We can observe it, we can admire it, and we can talk about it. But we don't readily appreciate that what we glibly call "the whirlpool" is not a particular thing. The whirlpool, shifting in the lake or on the river, doesn't hold its form. It becomes shallower; the molecules of water are in continuous change. In no two moments do we find the same configuration of water molecules defining the surface or shape of the whirlpool. Yet we view "the whirlpool" as a thing—as ice forming in fire.

We imagine enduring things, even as we think of "them" as fleeting. We hold to this notion at the expense of realizing that there's no actual thing there at all. We live in the clenched belief that ice actually does form in fire.

And what is *this* fire?

This fire is Mind—thoroughgoing movement, flux, flow, change. But since *all* is flux, Mind functions without anything actually moving.

If you attend very carefully, it becomes apparent that everything is like the whirlpool—not a thing at all, but change itself. If we could speed up our perspective enough, even a mass of stone would appear, over the course of millennia, to change and disappear, just like a whirlpool. (And if we could alter our perspective in the opposite way, we'd see the stone's constant molecular and atomic changes.)

But there's a far more subtle point here. It's only out of convention that I used the terms *stone* and *whirlpool*. Because, in fact, there is *only* change—*only* fire. There's no abiding thing called "stone" or "whirlpool" that changes. There's really no particular thing that's stone or whirlpool or you or me at all.

We think that the brittle icicles that form in our minds—icicles such as cats and stones and whirlpools and "me"—are actually the enduring, separate realities they appear to be. And then we focus our attention exclusively on those icicles.

But in doing so, we miss the fire—Mind—altogether. More important, we miss that even ice itself is purely fire.

41

PURELY MIND

THERE'S A LOT OF INTEREST in consciousness these days, and many recent books take up the topic. But what keeps coming across in these books is that we don't have a clear idea of what consciousness really is. Indeed, the whole conversation currently seems to be veering into discussions of matter—that is, brains, nerves, synapses, and such—rather than consciousness.

This is a little strange given that all of us are intimately familiar with consciousness. It's with us all the time. We can experience it and note it clearly in any moment we turn our attention to it. Yet we think of it as vague and mysterious.

Actually, we're just as confused about matter as we are about consciousness. For the most part, we consider matter to be the foundation of Reality itself.

Yet we have it all backward. If we look carefully and deeply, we can *see* that it's not mind or consciousness that's abstract but matter.

. . .

Matter is made of atoms. But what are atoms made of? When we move in closer to find out, we discover protons, neutrons, and electrons. We move closer still and discover that protons and neutrons are made of quarks. Yet none of these can pass for matter as we commonly think of it. Material entities have definite physical properties like mass, energy, location, and momentum. But electrons and other subatomic particles don't always have these attributes.

For example, we can't tell where an electron is unless we look for it. This doesn't seem odd until we note that when we find its current location, we now know nothing about its momentum (that is, the product of its mass, speed, and direction). So we look for its momentum instead. And we can find that, too, but only at the expense of knowing anything about its current location.

In other words, an electron doesn't seem to have properties that are separate from our awareness of those properties. Clearly, this is not matter as we commonly think of it—that is, as something substantive and separate from mind.

In fact, whenever we go looking at the stuff matter is made of, we find it inextricably enmeshed in consciousness. This observation prompted physicist and astronomer Sir Arthur Eddington to write, "Physics is the study of the structure of consciousness. The stuff of the world is mindstuff."

Other examples of the commingling of mind and matter abound. There's the famous double slit experiment in which electrons are fired toward a screen with two slits in it. When we don't try to identify which slit an electron travels through, we get a certain pattern, called a wave interference pattern, on the screen. But when we observe which slit the electron passes through, the pattern changes completely, to a diffraction pattern. Our simple awareness of which slit the electron uses profoundly changes the results of the experiment.

Our problems with matter stem from the fact that, unlike consciousness, which is directly experienced, matter is always secondary—that is, experienced indirectly, via mind. *This* is our actual, immediate, direct experience—it's purely mental, not physical.

In short, physical reality cannot be fully accounted for apart from consciousness. Yet it's not at all clear that matter is necessary to account for consciousness.

When we look at the physical world, we seem to see multiplicity: many things, all separate and distinct from each other, and all separate and distinct from "me," the observer. They also seem to exist apart from our personal, subjective experience of them.

Typically, what interests us in this view—let's call it View A—are all the seemingly separate and distinct objects. What we miss (or ignore or overlook) in this view is that all of these apparently separate objects work together to form an overall, Total picture.

In this view, we unquestioningly believe in the objectivity of that world "out there." We overlook actual experience and focus on the extremely seductive array of objects that appear in this ostensibly external world. Ultimately we're led to discard the actual experience of Totality in favor of what we can "objectively" measure, count, and quantify.

Thus we apply a variety of measurement tools to the vast array of objects that seem to appear in this external world, all in an effort to understand reality better. (These objects include not only shapes, colors, sounds, and smells, but also feelings, impressions, people, clouds, anger, love, confusion, passion, and so forth.) And so we develop an equally vast and seductive array of measurement tools.

But View A is a view of the world, not as we actually experience it, but as how we *think* we experience it. In other words, it's not the world as we perceive it but as we conceptualize it. And it's quite possible to understand this experience in another way.

In this second view, View B, it's the whole picture that is of interest to us, not the separate parts that make it up. Indeed, there do not appear to be any parts as such. In this second way of looking, the world is viewed not as multiplicity but as unity. The world is not seen as a huge collection of individual objects but as a single Whole. Often people who have had ecstatic and mystical experiences of Oneness or Unity confuse this view with enlightenment.

In the first view we find multiplicity and relativity; in the second, Oneness or Totality. Which view is correct?

In Zen we understand that to take hold of either view is to miss the mark. Although both views are indispensable, neither offers us an accurate picture of Reality.

The problem with the first view—View A, our commonsense view—is that it leads us into confusion. It's incapable of bringing us to any true Knowledge. The previous chapters of this book are replete with examples of how View A doesn't give us the whole picture.

But a common mistake among many religious practitioners, including many Buddhists, is to assume (or believe) that View B, Unity or Oneness, gives us a full and accurate view of Reality. But it doesn't, because it excludes View A, which clearly can't be denied. The world also appears as a multitude of things and thoughts.

The problem with these views is that they strike us as mutually exclusive. This is because, when we take hold of either one, we're caught up in conceptual thought. We're ignoring the immediate, direct experience of *this moment,* which includes *both views at once.* Clearly we experience multiplicity, and just as clearly, if we look carefully, we experience unity.

What's necessary to complete the picture is to *see* these two views, A and B, as merged—that is, as a single view.

A classic text by Zen teacher Shih-t'ou (Sekito Kisen) called the *Can Tong Qi (Sandokai),* "The Merging of Difference and Unity," points directly to this. In it there's a line that says, "Encountering Absolute is still not enlightenment."

When people first get a taste of Oneness they often think they've experienced enlightenment. This Oneness is a necessary realization, but it's not enlightenment, simply because Oneness does not account for the multiplicity that we encounter in every moment.

Truly *seeing* Reality is experiencing these two views at once so as to create a new, complete view.

Enlightenment is *seeing* that multiplicity (this everyday world of this and that) and unity (Oneness) are not two and cannot be made into two.

When we're locked on to View A alone, we have a hard time understanding, let alone explaining, consciousness. Holding tightly to View B is not much help, either. Unless we *see* both at once, we'll not understand consciousness. This is because consciousness itself *is* the dividing up of what is otherwise a seamless Whole. Both Oneness and multiplicity are necessary. They're not contradictory or mutually exclusive after all.

There's a fresh, direct, uncalculated, unconceptual way of realizing *this moment*. Once this is *seen*, we no longer rely so heavily or exclusively on our mental constructs—our thoughts, our beliefs, and our models of Reality. We not only *see* Views A and B as merged, we *see* that there was really only one view all along. This *seeing* is the sudden realization that there's a depth and dimension to our lives, and to the world, that we had been oblivious to.

To get a feeling for how this works, try out the simple exercise on the next page.

Hold the figure on the next page about twelve inches from your face. Stare at the two dots at the top of the figure, and let your eyes unfocus. Shift the book slightly until a third dot appears between the two. At this point, keep staring, but very slightly shift your vision downward until a three-dimensional image suddenly forms.

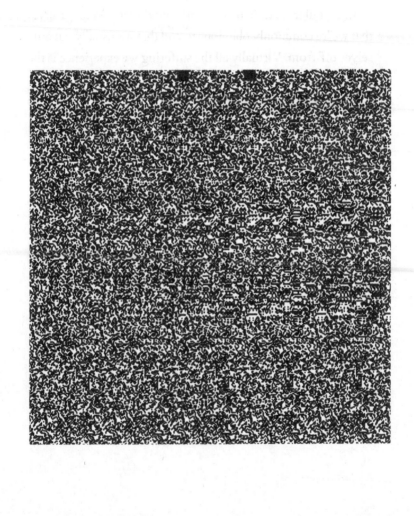

This image cannot be seen through our common way of approaching things, yet it leaps from the page the moment we know how to look for it.

In a similar way, there's a depth and dimension to our lives that we're commonly oblivious to and that we usually cut ourselves off from. Virtually all the suffering we experience is the result of cutting ourselves off in this way.

Yet what is necessary to free ourselves is right before our eyes at all times.

42

TIME AND NOW

I, the great earth, and all beings simultaneously
achieve the Way.

—The Buddha

Time is an illusion, albeit a persistent one.

—Albert Einstein

H OW COULD IT BE that the Buddha's enlightenment occurred simultaneously with all beings? Didn't this event happen a long time ago? If it already happened, where is it now? And doesn't "all beings" include us?

In Buddhist literature, many references point to a timeless-ness in things, relationships, and events. Nagarjuna, in a classic example, shows us that we can have no coherent conception of time as an entity. As he points out in his *Fundamentals of the Middle Way,* time can be experienced only as a set of interdependent relationships. Dogen draws this same insight to our attention in his essay "Being Time." Seng-ts'an, the third patriarch of Zen in China, ends his "Trusting the Heartmind" by telling us that "words fail, for the Way is neither yesterday, today, nor tomorrow." And in his classic "Merging of Difference and Unity," Zen teacher Shih-t'ou (Sekito Kisen) starts out by saying, "Mind is intimately communicated between east and west." Such an event must necessarily occur apart from any idea of time.

Nevertheless, we commonly look at the world, and our experience of the world, in a linear fashion, as if things were strung out in a line from past to present to future. Something that occurs now creates an effect later on. This, we think, is how things are and must be.

Which viewpoint is more in keeping with what science now offers us? And which one more accurately reflects how the world actually is?

Some physicists have recently taken a renewed interest in a peculiar way of conceptualizing time and space that has been around since the 1940s. One model of this view reduces the three dimensions of space to just two dimensions while projecting time in the third dimension.

According to this scheme, all of what we call "now"—that is, the arrangement of all things and events—is viewed as existing in a single, two-dimensional plane. Of course, this plane, being the present moment, doesn't stay put. Rather, it seems to rise upward through the third dimension (time), much like the floor of an elevator, except that in this case it ascends through time instead of through space. Within this conceptual model, the past is everything that has passed beneath the floor of the elevator in any given moment; the future—what's yet to come—is met when the floor of the elevator rises up to meet it.

In taking this view, we can imagine the whole of space-time as a three dimensional block and each entity as a point (or set of points) within that plane. Your life can be represented as the line you trace through this block as you ride the elevator up through time.

Some physicists see this as a way to account for consciousness as well. As mathematical physicist Herman Weyl described it, "The objective world simply is; it does not happen. Only to the gaze of my consciousness, crawling upward along the life line of my body, does a section of this world come to life as a fleeting image which continuously changes in time."

But why should we think of time as movement at all?

In devising the above scheme, and in examining temporal phenomena in general, physicists of course have continued to hold the commonsense assumption that time is still a movement from past to present to future. But maintaining this view presents some problems. For example, physicists have discovered that certain quantum events seem to ride the elevator down instead of up.

Specifically, science has had to account for a particle called a positron. This is not some theoretical or hypothetical entity but an actual particle that shows up in a number of quantum experiments. A positron can be seen as either a positively charged electron (except that electrons are negatively charged) or an electron running backward in time. As we shall see in a moment, the second view solves a variety of puzzling problems that have stumped physicists for some time.

The simplest solution, of course, would be to forget any apparent nonsense about there being entities that can run backward in time, since such entities can just as easily be seen, from a mathematical point of view, as running "forward" in time as well. Many physicists, in fact, have tried to do just that. The problem was that when they began conceiving positrons as electrons traveling from the future through the present to the past, their overall picture of the universe suddenly became greatly simplified. For physicists, this simplicity provides a strong incentive for taking things seriously. Moreover, by looking at things in this temporally backward way, they've recently discovered that they're able to conceptualize many quantum phenomena they could not otherwise explain— phenomena that utterly baffled them for decades.

But accepting such a scheme leads us to a lot of *other* puzzling things. For one thing, it means, in a very real sense, that the universe doesn't have any size or duration. It means that we have the Whole of Reality—all of time, all of space—at once.

In other words, nothing rides up or down the time elevator tracing out lines at all—not our bodies, not consciousness, not positrons. In fact, there *isn't* any such line of time. It's an illusion, and it's the focus of our confusion about time.

. . .

In highly simplified terms, physicists are beginning to hypothesize something like this. When, say, an electron in your kitchen vibrates, it sends out a signal traveling at the speed of light through all of time and space. When another electron receives that signal, it vibrates sympathetically and sends a return signal back to the original electron in your kitchen. Each electron gets this information from other particles everywhere—indeed, from literally everything that it reaches out to touch in all of time and space. As a result of this process, each electron "knows" its exact place and importance in the universe.

Let's take a closer look at this. Say we excite an electron here within this page (let's call it the sender). It sends out a signal (that is, it emits a photon traveling in wave form) at the speed of light into the universe. It might go no farther than the width of this page, or it might travel to the Andromeda Galaxy two million light-years away. But it doesn't matter where or how far it goes because sooner or later the photon will be absorbed by some other electron (which we'll call the responder). That electron vibrates in response and sends a return signal back to the sender electron here within this page.

According to our commonsense view, if the signal goes to Andromeda, which is two million light-years away, it would take four million years for the signal to get back to the sender in this page.

But it seems (and many experiments have borne this out) that *the responder's return signal is received by the sender at the same moment the sender first sends out its signal.* Instead of taking four million years for the signal to go to Andromeda and return, the entire transaction takes place *simultaneously.* Not in a microsecond *but in the exact same moment.*

In other words, the whole transaction happens *now,* apart from time. *Now,* instead of time.

Some physicists explain this phenomenon by saying that when the responder receives a signal, it sends its return signal backward in time. And since it takes exactly as much time for a signal to return as it does to go out, the whole affair is complete in the same moment it began. Physicists have real experimental data that support such an explanation, which they call the "transactional interpretation of quantum mechanics."

Furthermore, if we look at this transaction from the standpoint of the signals themselves, no time at all elapses during the entire supposed four-million-year journey. Einstein showed us that if we could somehow get ourselves up to the speed of light (unlike photons, we have mass, so we can't really do this, but let's be hypothetical for a moment), time would slow down as our velocity increased (though it would not appear so to us), until finally, at the speed of light, time would cease to elaspse at all. From the standpoint of someone traveling at the speed of light, it would appear that *all* the space being traversed— every inch or light-year of it—would pass by at once, no matter how long the journey might be.

So, from the viewpoint of a photon going to Andromeda, the journey takes literally no time at all. In other words, to the photon, Andromeda is right *here*, since it takes no time whatsoever to get "there." And the fact that the message is there and here simultaneously makes "there" indistinguishable from "here."

This would be equally true for *any* two "locations" in the universe that you could point to.

In other words, the universe doesn't appear to have any intrinsic size or duration at all.

To our everyday mind, the universe is unimaginably vast and ancient beyond reckoning. But to the enlightened person, no attempt is made to qualify (or quantify) an objective Reality in such ways.

As Huang Po, a great Zen teacher from ninth-century China, said, "It is without beginning, unborn, and indestructible. It cannot be thought of in terms of new or old. It is neither long nor short, big nor small, for it transcends all limits, measures, names, traces, and comparisons."

The Universe—as *seen* by the awakened—has neither an intrinsic size nor age. All there is is *here* and *now*.

Nevertheless, within this *here* and *now*, which has no extension or duration in space or time, we seem to have dimensions of space and time. How, then, can space and time occur at all?

They appear as the result of consciousness.

It's only in our mental construction of the universe—our conception of it—that we encounter something vast and enduring. In our actual experience, however—that is, what we actually *perceive* rather than conceive of—all we ever have is *here* and *now*.

Our experience is always in the present. We literally cannot exist in the future or past, only in the timeless moment of infinitely short duration that we call *now*. We only remember the past and imagine the future, but both of these activities necessarily occur *now*.

And where can you ever possibly be but *here*? *Here* we conceive of a "there," but you cannot actually go there. No matter where you "go," you never leave *here*.

What we experience as duration and extension—time and space—results from the way Mind operates. Consciousness produces them. Indeed, this is what consciousness *is*. Consciousness is the division of *this* otherwise seamless Whole, which transcends space and time, *into* space and time—that is, into here and there, then and now.

It's the various mental constructions that we hold, and hold dear, that appear as time and space, extension and duration. These—and all of the material world—derive from consciousness, which ladles out time and space from a timeless, spaceless sea.

To the awakened, however, what is Real is this seamless, boundless, spaceless, timeless Whole. The enlightened person *sees* that this Whole doesn't have any dimension apart from Mind.

43

ENLIGHTENMENT

I F WE TALK about enlightenment too much, we can get the
idea that it's a special state of mind that is worth pursuing
at all costs. Then we end up striving for it, believing that it will
provide us with something wonderful: insight, bliss, ecstasy,
release, freedom from pain.

But enlightenment is not like this at all. Words like *bliss* and
ecstasy don't apply. These are terms we put on ordinary experiences. And enlightenment doesn't belong in that category.

Thinking highly (or longingly) of enlightenment is just
another form of delusion. Yet it's a trap that some Zen practitioners easily fall into. It's easy to get worked up over the
thought of enlightenment. But this is the wrong approach.
We're better off having no thought of enlightenment at all.

In fact, enlightenment isn't much more than remembering
something long forgotten that's been with you all along.

So teachers in the Soto Zen tradition avoid making a big
deal out of enlightenment. But in doing so, we tend to err in the
opposite direction. We rarely bring up the subject, or we treat

enlightenment as if it were taboo. If it's mentioned at all, we seem to speak of it in hushed tones. Thus we inadvertently teach a kind of uneasiness in discussing it.

This leads to a great deal of unnecessary confusion, and it gives people the completely incorrect impression that enlightenment is vague, mysterious, and difficult (or impossible) to realize.

What's wrong with this picture? Where do all this confusion, difficulty, and misunderstanding come from? Why should there be any problem here at all? Why can't this matter of enlightenment be clearly defined and understood like any other concern?

It rarely occurs to us that there's something wrong with the questions we commonly ask about enlightenment. These questions typically come from very basic, common misunderstandings that in turn derive from fragmented, dualistic thinking.

First of all, enlightenment is not an ecstatic or blissful state. There are moments, certainly, when we're smitten with some sudden insight or clarity of mind. These may be quite genuine and even very powerful. In Zen we call each such moment a *kensho,* which is a Japanese word. These experiences may help you sort out your life or give you a sense of direction or assist you in your daily Zen practice, but such things in themselves are no indication of enlightenment.

Sometimes *kensho* experiences may involve ecstatic feelings, but then so may other experiences like falling in love or listening to music. And while it's been said that after moments of ecstasy there will still be laundry to do, this is not true about enlightenment.

This is because there *is* no "after enlightenment." Enlightenment lies beyond any idea of time. Any temporal notions we have about enlightenment come from our dualistic understanding.

The Buddha, who was well acquainted with ecstatic moments and blissful states, spoke of such things as not being enlightenment. This is because, like everything else that we can name or describe or conceptualize, they don't last. Eventually we come out of them, back to Earth. And when we do, we have to face the laundry. It was real ecstasy, sure, but it wasn't enlightenment.

Something else takes place with enlightenment, however, that's got nothing to do with ecstasy, and from which you don't emerge. This is because what is finally realized is that there was no "you" to go into enlightenment in the first place. Thus everything about waking up is wholly different from entering (or leaving) a state of bliss.

If there's some particular thing you can name, pick up, single out, or point to, it's not enlightenment; it's ordinary. It's not true liberation or freedom of mind.

The twenty-seventh case of the Zen text the *Blue Cliff Record* sheds some light on this matter. A student asks Zen teacher Yun Men, "When the tree withers and the leaves fall, what then?" Yun Men answers, "The body is visible in the autumn wind."

Yun Men is pointing out that whenever we think we actually have something, if we look at it carefully, we can *see* that it withers and dies. Whatever you want to carve out and put in front of you—your reputation, your training and experience, your very life, even the teachings of the Buddha—they all wither, die, and pass away. Whatever it is, if it's separated out from the Whole, it will wither and die. There's no point in pretending that conditions are (or ever will be) otherwise.

But this only appears sad, depressing, and nihilistic to us when we hold to the notion that we actually had something solid and persisting in the first place.

After years of practicing Zen, people sometimes wonder, "What's it all for? What good has this been? What have I—or the world, for that matter—gotten out of it?" But this is just another form of perpetuating and aggrandizing an imaginary self.

If we *look* carefully, we can *see* that there's no particular thing persisting, even *now*. There never has been and never will be—nor could there be.

If we understand this "no particularness," we won't be confused on this issue about becoming or being enlightened. Nor will we be baffled and depressed when we hear the more profound utterances on the subject, such as Yun Men's.

To the extent that we have something, anything at all, including a sense of self, it dies. Were we to actually *see* this, we'd be liberated immediately.

What do you truly and completely have or own or control? What have you ever had?

To the awakened, having is simply not what life is about.

. . .

Tenkei, an eighteenth-century Japanese Zen teacher of the Soto tradition, commented on Yun Men's tree this way: "What season is this when the tree withers and dies? When eating and drinking, what time is it?"

In other words, what season and time is it *now?* If we look carefully, we can *see* that nothing holds still. There's nothing static at all in actual experience. All is flux. There's no particular point in time or space that we can pin down or identify unambiguously. There's only *now.*

It's always *now.* We can never move away from *now* or get beyond it. And *now* isn't any particular time at all.

And all those seemingly real things we cling to and possess—most notably ourselves—aren't anything in particular, either.

We typically think there's only one of "me" and that this singular "me" persists, at least for a time. But actually, in each moment, there's someone new. Moods change; thoughts change; concerns change; the very molecules and atoms that make up what you call "my body" change. There's no particular person who is "you." We may think there is, but when we *look* closely enough, we don't find one.

This is what Huang Po was talking about when he said that the wise—the awakened—reject what they think, not what they *see.*

We think there is a particular, enduring person here, and then we wonder, "Is this person enlightened?" or "Will I ever become enlightened?" But there is no particular person who becomes enlightened—or who remains deluded. All such questions are off the mark.

I received a letter from a Zen student who wanted to know why some Zen teachers won't tell you if they're enlightened, even when asked directly. It's a valid question. The reason teachers often won't say yes or no is this: a teacher who *is* awake realizes that there's no particular person who's awake. Thus answering either yes or no to the question would validate the premise that there's a particular person being referred to, which is not the case. Thus neither yes nor no is an appropriate response to the question.

This is not to say that there are no awakened people. There are. But they're awakened in *this moment;* they're not the enduring entities we imagine them to be.

What *does* appear is like the formation of the swirl of air that rolls from the butterfly as it flaps its wings. Most of the swirls that spin off the butterfly's wings die or are absorbed into other gusts, but "this swirl" appears to grow. It takes on the energy of other swirls in the wind. Eventually, if "it" becomes big enough, we give it a name like Cindy or Bob. Once given a name, it seems more particular and enduring. It appears to have a life of its own.

A hurricane moves. It changes, it grows, and it dies. But what, exactly, was Hurricane Bob or Cindy? No particular thing at all. In every stage, at every moment, what we call Bob or Cindy or you or me is nothing in particular, yet it's formed of the energy of the Whole.

We're like whirlpools and music, hurricanes and icicles. Once formed—that is, conceived—we're seemingly particular things, yet in each moment, all is fresh and new.

Thus, when you ask an enlightened person if they're

enlightened, be prepared to get a Yogi Berra–like response. (When asked, "Hey, Yogi, what time is it?" he allegedly retorted, "You mean now?")

We wonder about enlightenment. We want to know who's got it, what it's like, and if we can get it ourselves. But a better question to ask would be, "Who wants to know?"

One more point needs to be made with regard to enlightenment: when we're caught up in concepts, in particularity, we unwittingly sell ourselves short—and put a great deal of effort into doing so. This is a very quiet but deeply insidious trap in which we easily get caught. Here's how it works.

We habitually take the wrong approach to enlightenment, which is assuming that we need an approach. We don't. Indeed, taking an approach keeps us and enlightenment forever separated.

As soon as we take an approach, we create something to be approached—something "out there." But enlightenment isn't "out there." It can't be approached. It's already *here, now.* Enlightenment is neither particular nor graspable—yet it's always available to perception.

You might still feel it would be nice if you could take hold of something and say, "This is It! This is what I want. This is what I need." But at some point you must truly realize—viscerally, and not through mere intellection—that all such pointlike things wither and die. They do not satisfy; they do not still the deep ache of the heart.

There's no mystery until you grasp. If you don't override immediate experience with your personal longings and loathings, if you recall an earnest desire to get to the bottom of this matter regarding human delusion, though there's no particular thing you need to look for, you'll recognize Reality and Truth.

Just don't suppose that there's any place you can cast your eyes and not gaze upon Reality and Truth.

REALITY IS NOT
WHAT YOU THINK

Whatever you think is delusion.

—Dainin Katagiri

THE PERCEPTION of an awakened person is identical to your own.

It's a good thing, too, because this means *you* can awaken. All that is necessary is to *see* Reality, directly. We only need to get beyond our calculating mind, our thinking mind, our explaining mind.

Our confusion is only the result of what we think. Reality doesn't need any explanation whatsoever. In fact, it can't be explained. And it doesn't need to be; after all, it's already *here*. Explanations are merely an attempt to say what Reality is like. But it's absurd to think that Reality could be like anything.

Reality isn't *like* anything. It's Reality. Reality itself is inconceivable—it won't go into a conceptual package. But it doesn't need to. We already *see* it. We simply need to stop trying to take hold of it.

Whatever you hold to, let it go. Step into *this moment*. Come back to *just this*. It takes some effort. But come back, come back, come back to *just this*. *Just see* what you've been ignoring for so long.

ACKNOWLEDGMENTS

My sincere thanks to Cathy Brooks, Hank Brooks, Doreen Gunderson Dunn, Bev Forsman, Al Jacobson, S. Evan Jones, Kathy Kvern, Cassandra O'Malley, John Vieira, and Kay Hanson for transcribing many of the talks that formed the basis of this book. Kay also coordinated the transcription of these talks.

Let me reserve a special thank-you, however, for Sharon Plett, who transcribed more than half of the pieces that went into this volume. Indeed, Sharon produces transcripts nearly as fast as I deliver my talks.

Thanks also to Daniel Boemer, Christa Cerra, Ann O'Fallon, and Mary Olympia, who also produced transcripts. Ultimately, I decided not to use them here, but they will likely be used in future books.

One transcript used for this book was done by someone who left no indication of who they were. I'd like to acknowledge their efforts here.

Thanks also to my longtime friend Clarence Douville and my Dharma brother Norm Randolph, whose careful readings of the manuscript yielded several improvements and corrections.

Thanks to my Dharma brother Nonin Chowaney, who told me a version of the story of the teachable and less-teachable students that appears in chapter 31.

I am grateful to Irvin Rock and his book, *Perception*, for the idea behind the map in chapter 13.

Thanks to my wife, Jean, for her untiring support, her sound advice, and the translation of Jacques Prévert in chapter 7.

My profound thanks to Jose Palmieri, who has assisted me in countless way these past few years and who created all the graphics that appear in this book.

And finally, as always, my deep thanks to Scott Edelstein, my literary agent, editor, and friend of many years, without whose efforts and know-how none of my writings would likely have ever seen the light of day.

ABOUT THE AUTHOR

Steve Hagen is a longtime teacher of Buddhism and the author of *Buddhism Plain and Simple* and *How the World Can Be the Way It Is.*

Hagen began studying Buddhism in 1967 and in 1975 became a student of Zen master Dainin Katagiri, author of *Returning to Silence* and *You Have to Say Something.* Hagen was ordained in 1979 and later studied with a number of other teachers in Asia and Europe. In 1989 he received Dharma transmission (endorsement to teach) from Katagiri Roshi.

Hagen lives in Minneapolis, where he is head teacher at Dharma Field Meditation and Learning Center. He is currently working on several other books.

Recordings of courses and talks by Steve Hagen on Buddhism and Zen are available by mail and e-mail.

For a list of topics and prices, go to Dharma Field's Web site at

www.dharmafield.org

or send a self-addressed, stamped envelope to:

Dharma Field Zen Center

3118 West 49th Street

Minneapolis, MN 55410